Samoan Queer Lives

Dan Taulapapa McMullin
and
Yuki Kihara

with
Tuilagi Seiuli Ailani Allan Alo Va`ai
Resitara Apa
Brian Fuata
Matautia Phineas Hartson
Memea Eleitino Ma`aelopa
Shevon Solipo Kaio Matai
Jean Melesaine
Sal Salamaotua Tatupu Poloai
Kiana Rivera
Isaako Si`uleo
Tootooali`i Roger Stanley
Taualeo`o Stephen Stehlin
Alex Su`a
Ireneo Tauailauti Veavea

little island press

Samoan Queer Lives was first
published in 2018 by little island press

Text copyright © 2018 Dan Taulapapa McMullin and Yuki Kihara
Dan Taulapapa McMullin and Yuki Kihara assert their moral rights
to be identified as the authors of this work.

With photographs from the collections of Fa`afafine Associations,
historical collections and personal collections of the participating contributors.

Additional photographs by Evotia Tamua

Format copyright © 2018 little island press limited

Published by little island press,
P. O. Box 6786, Wellesley Street,
Auckland 1141, New Zealand
www.littleisland.co.nz

201901181751

ISBN 978-1-877484-27-8

A catalogue record for this book is available from the
National Library of New Zealand.

Royalties from the sale of this book
will be donated to fa`afafine groups
in Sāmoa and Sāmoa Amelika.

The book was produced with assistance from Creative New Zealand
and UCLA Postcolonial Theory & Literary Studies Group.

ARTS COUNCIL
NEW ZEALAND TOI AOTEAROA
creative*nz*

In memory of
Shevon Solipo Kaio Matai
Tuilagi Seiuli Ailani Allan Alo Va`ai
Memea Eleitino Ma`aelopa
Tootooali`i Roger Stanley

Contents

Yuki Kihara
Photographer: Greg Semu

Foreword

Yuki Kihara

On Monday 27 June 2016 an early morning candlelight procession was held in Apia, the capital of Sāmoa, on ʻUpolu, led by members of the Sāmoa Faʻafafine Association (SFA). They were holding candles and banners with messages such as 'End Media Violation of Faʻafafine', 'Social Justice and Peace', and 'End Violence and Discrimination of Faʻafafine'. The banners were directed at a controversy over the *Sunday Samoan*'s reporting of the death of Jeanine Tuivaiki, a 20-year-old computer student and faʻafafine who died of a suspected suicide. The *Sāmoa Observer* published an unblurred photograph on the front page after her death and referred to Tuivaiki as male in its coverage. The reportage sent shockwaves across Sāmoa, especially given that the faʻafafine community had recently celebrated repeal of the Crimes Ordinance 1961, a law enforced during the New Zealand colonial administration of Sāmoa that criminalised 'the impersonation of a female' by any male in Sāmoa. The law was used to persecute faʻafafine with fines or imprisonment as the penalty, although the police stopped enforcing it in the early 1980s. The SFA said the repeal of the law was 'a huge celebration for the faʻafafine community and vindication for families who have lost members to acts of violence'.

Today the social equilibrium that has long existed across the gender spectrum prior to missionisation has been greatly disturbed by religious conservatism, which operates an inflammatory televangelism channel in Sāmoa. Faʻafafine are used as scapegoats by religious leaders, who increasingly blame homosexuality, HIV/AIDS and even climate change on fa`afafine, whenever society is under social, political, cultural and economic pressure from the West.

Fa`afafine have become a 'hot' topic in the West, in contrast to Western identity; this is echoed in the works of contemporary Western documentary filmmakers, anthropologists and travel writers in search of fa`afafine with a 'primitive' gender and sexuality, living close to 'nature', as measured against the 'civilised' Western cisgendered heteronormative patriarchy.

As fa`afafine have been affected by streams of colonisers since the seventeenth century, in contrast to Western essentialist stereotypes, I've coined the terms 'fa`afaphobia' to describe prejudices aimed at fa`afafine in the postcolonial era, and 'fa`afafeminism' to reflect on our intersection with feminist issues.

Samoan Queer Lives delves into the unique lives of Samoan people who are 'fa`afafine' – broadly understood in the Western interpretation as persons who are of transgender, intersexed and third sex, or gay, lesbian and bisexual origin. Following on from a long history of anthropological studies, travel journals and documentaries on Sāmoa that too often distort or sensationalise fa`afafine life, this publication– the first of its kind, edited and written by fa`afafine – provides a vehicle for historical perspective. Here fa`afafine share their stories in their own words. The book provides personal accounts that cross lines of gender and culture, and span generations, professions and geography to include fa`afafine based in independent Sāmoa, the US Territory of American Sāmoa, Aotearoa New Zealand, Australia, the Kingdom of Hawai`i, and Turtle Island–United States of America.

Each life history chapter in the book is accompanied by a portrait selected from the participants' personal collection. In the process of recording and editing these histories, the editors draw on Samoan communal social practise of tala or history and talanoaga or conversation. We aim to examine how history and the subject are defined from a contemporary Samoan perspective in the experience of fa`afafine living in Sāmoa and the diaspora.

Each chapter is a picture of the immediate environment of their homes, families, partners, friends, workplaces – from the islands, now the place of eternal return, to the alluring lights of the city, now home. The stories are by turns angry, humorous, intimate and raw. *Samoan Queer Lives* addresses Western stereotypes of transgenders and gays, while exposing challenges fa`afafine face as a traditional class in a changing Samoan society.

We would like to thank all the contributors who generously offered to tell their personal stories in the publication that aims to offer a better understanding of our diverse lives as Samoans and as fa`afafine and queer peoples. Over the course of working on this publication, four of our friends and contributors to this publication passed away and will not have the chance to see this publication to fruition. Our thoughts are with them and their loved ones.

I would also like to thank our co-editor and writer Dan Taulapapa McMullin for his expertise and hard work interviewing, transcribing and editing the chapters and photographs. And my thanks go to Little Island Press for believing in this publication; and to Creative New Zealand Arts Council for travel funds in the research phase.

As the topic of fa`afafine continues to gain momentum in international media and academic scholarship that too often deals with the enigmatic question 'What is a fa`afafine?', *Samoan Queer Lives* address a more pertinent question: 'What is life?'

Yuki Kihara,
creative producer and co-editor
of *Samoan Queer Lives*

Portrait of a fa`afafine from Tutuila with hair bound in a topknot.
American Sāmoa, circa 1860s
Photographer: John Davis
Museum of Archaeology and Anthropology, P.4740.ACH1

Introduction:
Fa`afafine Studies

Dan Taulapapa McMullin

The photograph seems to have no history but its surface: a photograph of a Samoan man with a topknot, taken at a time when topknots and turbans were fading from use by Samoan men as protection in war – a couple of generations after Christianisation, when Samoan men were made by the new church to cut their long hair short; when Samoan women were made to change 'pagan' short hair styles to the long hair preferred by Christian women, like a veil. And unlike most Samoan warrior colonial photographs popular at the time, he does not carry a war club.

Shevon Matai, to whose memory we dedicate this book, said in her memoir:

> I think I want to say that fa`afafine are fascinating creatures and their lives are lived on the surface and they belong to be lived on the surface of life ... I believe that you don't have to look too far to understand who we are because it's right there you just have to have the right eye.

The meaning of the photograph is open to interpretation. Our history as fa`afafine is in our way of seeing. In her auto-biography, which influenced this book, fa`afafine educator Vena Sela wrote, 'Not much was written by the early missionaries about fa`afafines because there was no significant impression of a different lifestyle. There were fa`afafines but they all looked

Chiefs and Chiefesses Passing on Their Way
to a Great Conference, Evening, Samoa
John La Farge, 1891
The Athanaeum, United States
This image is in the public domain.

the same to the missionaries: primitive natives, pagans and uncivilised.'[1]

In the nineteenth century, given Western secular and religious laws against transgenders and homosexuals, how could European missionaries write on lives that might reflect their own secret desires?

In 1891 American painter John LaFarge, with fellow American writer Henry Adams, went on a world tour that included Tahiti and Sāmoa, just before Paul Gauguin began his own journeys in Polynesia. Among LaFarge's many painting sketches in Sāmoa is one entitled, 'Chiefs and Chiefesses Passing on Their Way to a Great Conference. Evening. Samoa.' Except none of the 'chiefesses' seem to have women's breasts, and all the chiefs seem to walk with a certain exaggerated grace.

One of the very few nineteenth-century references to fa`afafine is in the Samoan dictionary of 1862–1911 by Reverend George Pratt of the London Missionary Society, who arrived in Sāmoa in 1839. Pratt translates the English word 'effeminate' as 'amio fa`afafine' or 'to conduct oneself in the way of a woman.' However, he translates fa`afafine as 'a hermaphrodite'; and 'belonging to women, as some kinds of work.'

The word fa`afafine is not mentioned in the Tusi Paia,[2] the Samoan Bible, translated in 1862 by Pratt with others. Regarding transgenderism, in Teuteronome, Moses in the King James version was translated: 'Aua ne`i ofu le fafine i le ofu o le tane; aua foi le ofu le tane i le ofu o le fafine ...'[3] Perhaps the saving grace for fa`afafine is that we are neither fafine (women-wives) nor tane (men-husbands). So, strictly speaking, in word and spirit, linguistically and culturally, fa`afafine are passed over in the Bible.

The term fa`afafine was, until recently, a Samoan word

---

1   Vanessa, *Memoirs of a Samoan, Catholic, and Fa'afafine*, 2007.
2   Published in full in 1884.
3   Deuteronomy, XXII, 5: 'The woman shall not wear that which pertaineth unto a man, neither shall a man put on a woman's garment.'

encompassing all queer LGBT Samoan people, including gay men, lesbians, and female to male transgenders, as well as male to female transgenders. Fa`afafine was used as a postcolonial transition word, a liminal space encompassing all genders and sexualities, not in opposition to heteropatriarchy, but not in equilibrium with it either. Like much Samoan thinking it is not binary and oppositional, but bilateral and reciprocal.

Tauatāne is defined as 'homosexual acts between men' in linguist G.B Milner's Samoan Dictionary, published in 1966.[4] However in Pratt's dictionary of 100 years earlier, tauatāne is defined as 'v.1. To have dancing with men only. 2. To engage in fight with men, i.e., brave men'. And, 's. a species of sodomy, *sed non introiens*.'[5] A common form of sexual expression among men and fa`afafine in Sāmoa is intercrural[6] or `auaga or pipi `auaga.[7]

The word fa'atane, 'in the manner of a man', first appears in print in 1879 in Le Père Louis Violette's French–Samoan–English dictionary as 'comme un homme, en parlant d'une femme (as a man)' (when speaking of a woman).[8] Fa'atane then shows up in Pratt's 1898 third edition of his Samoan–English dictionary as 'fa`atane, v. to be masculine, of a woman'.[9] The term fa`atane does not appear in Milner's 1966 dictionary at all.

The slang word 'mala' for fa`afafine, which is falling out of use, is generally considered to be related to the meaning attributed to it in the Tusi Pa`ia: a calamity, a misfortune, a plague. The usage of this word for fa`afafine might have coincided with the rise in HIV/AIDS and fundamentalism.

---

4 Milner was commissioned to compile and publish Samoan Dictionary by the Governments of Western Sāmoa and American Sāmoa, 1966.
5 Latin: 'but not entering'.
6 Insertion between thighs, common among Polynesians, and also with the ancient Greeks.
7 Thighs or pussy thighs; 'pipi' is a kind of small pretty shell and shellfish.
8 Louis Violette, Dictionnaire Samoa–Français–Anglais et Français–Samoa-Anglais (Paris: Maisonneuve, 1879).
9 George Pratt, A Grammar and Dictionary of the Samoan Language, 3rd edn (London Missionary Society, 1893).

The change of meaning in the time between these dictionaries seems to indicate a change in public discourse among Samoans. Under the influence of biblical law, Samoan language changed as well. In the Tusi Paia in Korinito (where Paul is translated from the King James English translation) tauatane is used for 'effeminate', and receptive lovers are 'faasotoma' or Sodomites: 'Aua ne'i faaseseina outou; o e faitaga, ma e ifo i tupua, ma e mulilulua, ma e tauātane, ma e faasotoma.'[10]

Tauatāne could literally be translated as war-husband or precious-man. In its biblical and missionary reference the indigenous meaning was changed, or removed. Today tauatāne is not in common use. Translation appropriates meaning, it changes the meaning of indigenous words, it Westernises their meaning, it sometimes divests them of their original meaning. It is a kind of mirror of the West. The authority that Western writers use in commenting on fa'afafine is based on a sense of difference that too often lacks nuance – what Tuiatua Tamasese calls the 'fragrance' of indigenous reference.[11]

In the twentieth century, when numbers of American sailors and soldiers encountered fa'afafine and other gender and sexual expressions in the Pacific during World War Two, they responded with a kind of joyful and privileged appropriation. These appropriations by Americans, a sort of queer tiki kitsch, had an influence on what would come to be, within a generation, the beginnings of the gay liberation movement in America. The history of gay liberation was based in part on the erasure of indigenous two-spirit[12] histories; it required their erasure to ensure a place in the existing sexual hierarchy of colonialism.

The word fa'afatama is hybrid under the influence of English on Samoan language; it is recent and listed in neither Pratt nor Milner's dictionaries. Fatama is a combination of fafine

---

10 I Corinthians VI, 9: 'Be not deceived: neither fornicators, nor idolators, nor adulterers, nor effeminate, nor abusers of themselves with mankind ...'

11 Tuiatua Tamasese, Su'esu'e Manogi: In search of fragrance, 2008.

12 Two-spirit: Native American expression for transgender or LGBT.

Dan Taulapapa McMullin
Photographer: Stephen Dunn

or woman-wife and tama or boy-child-chief. Fa`afatama is a translation of the English 'tomboy', or 'the way of a tomboy', into Samoan. It is a gender role that is as precolonial as fa`afafine, but whose meaning and form are influenced by colonialism.

The suppression of fa`afāfine, tauatāne, fa`atane, and fa`afatama reflects the influence of Westernisation and monotheism on Samoan society. This is connected to the influence of the West on the roles of women in Samoan society. In images of Samoan traditional warfare in the nineteenth century, women carrying war clubs mingle with men – and often stand in the foreground as warriors. In warfare during nineteenth-century colonialism, where only Samoan men are carrying guns, Samoan women are usually displayed carrying water, their figures turned away in submission.

Missionaries coming to Sāmoa and American Sāmoa were very concerned with outlawing any form of cohabitation, or relationships outside of marriage as within the church. This is reflected today in the current colonially founded laws against sodomy and marriage equality. One of the translations of fa`afafine is 'the way of a wife', and fa`atane 'the way of a husband'; marriage equality is woven into the language of Sāmoa, although at the moment it is outlawed.

The eternal child is a concept that also impinges on Western viewpoints that influence Samoan society, especially in regard to notions about native tradition and what many Samoans piously refer to as 'the culture', as something outgrown – as something for children, tamaiti, to outgrow as they become tagata, humans.

In all these categories of personhood – fa`afafine, tauatāne, fa`atane, fa`afatama, fafine, āvā, tamaiti and tagata[13] – there was a shift, one that attempted to erase fa`afafine, tauatāne, and fa`atane and, in that attempt, changed how we saw ourselves.

---

13   In Pratt's 1862 dictionary tagata is defined as: '1. A man. 2. Mankind. 3. A servant.' In Milner's 1966 dictionary tagata is defined as: '1. A man (i.e. human being of either sex, person). 2. Native (The __ of Africa). 3. Prisoner of war.'

The Sāmoa Islands has a history of several thousand years, at times united, as during the height of the power of the Tui Manuʻa in Sāmoa's distant past, and at times divided politically, as it was in the 1890s when the United States took military control over the eastern islands or American Sāmoa; and when Germany and later New Zealand took control over the western islands, now independent Sāmoa. After World War Two, Samoans began migrating en masse to Aotearoa New Zealand and Australia from Sāmoa, and to Hawaiʻi and the United States from American Sāmoa. The writings in this book are representative of this Samoan diaspora but, as the reader will find, boundaries are a matter of personal history, they can be as limitless as our genders. One etymology of the word Sāmoa is the family *Sā* of the center *Moa*; or, in another frequent form, *Samoana*, the family Sā of the ocean Moana – we are both the land of our ancestors and the seas that surround us.

The stories in *Samoan Queer Lives* are based on interviews we conducted throughout the Samoan diaspora in Australia, Aotearoa New Zealand, Fiji, Hawaiʻi and the United States, as well as the moa, the center, in independent Sāmoa and American Sāmoa, along with two plays – *Faʻafafine* by Brian Fuata in Australia and *Puzzy* by Kiana Rivera in Hawaiʻi. We attempted to keep the voices of our collaborators intact, and this Introduction expresses just one viewpoint among the many in this book. We hope with this book to further the discourse on faʻatane, faʻafatama, tauātane, tane, fafine, and faʻafafine, and about what it is to be tagata Sāmoa and tagata Moana.

These interviews include many different kinds of personal journeys within many quite different Samoan communities around the world. This was made possible by the honesty, warmth, critical enquiry, humour and insightful awareness of our collaborators. It is in that shared space between us that the theme of this book resides.

In his mémoire, which opens this collection, choreographer and director Ailani Alo spoke about the Polynesian concepts of mana and vā, which Samoans often speak of when we say 'teuga o le vā'– take care of this space between us:

> Go with my mana. Mana is more than power. Mana is more than essence as well. Mana is my connections and that's not just physical or mental or emotional but spiritual as well.

Tuilagi Seiuli Ailani Allan Alo Va`ai
Photographer: Evotia Tamua

Tuilagi Seiuli Ailani Allan Alo Va`ai

I've never really tried to be either a girl or a guy. I've always been me. And I suppose being me is fa`afafine. Then, all of the expression I put in my work is I. It's not colored by any gender of any kind. I've never been cautious of what is man or woman, how I see my perspective of any situation, and it was not ever politicised or in a contest where a fa`afafine or a man or a woman is treated in any way.

The awareness of being fa`afafine has always influenced and colored my struggle as an artist because when I first started my parents never wanted me to do any dancing or any artistic thing. Actually they wanted me to be a lawyer. I changed my whole focus of study because to be a lawyer was to be caged in. And to be a lawyer was to be a man or a woman.

To be an artist is to be me, or fa`afafine. It allowed for the platform to be free – to express who I was and how I really saw the world. For me it was a retaliatory position to what the norm was. And I suppose I was in a way struggling to be free and at the same time trying to create a career path in the arts in dance and theatre. And I believe I did. I came at the right place at the right time.

When Epeli Hau`ofa[1] was here[2] – he treated me like who I was because he did not judge me. He did not try to change my expression. He nurtured me in that he just said, 'There's your space; let me know if you need anything. Otherwise, go for it.' So in a way, I came to USP at the right time when I needed a

---

1 Tongan writer Epeli Hau`ofa (1939–2009).

2 Oceania Centre for Arts, Culture and Pacific Studies, University of the South Pacific, Suva, Fiji, where Alo was creative director. He later became regional outreach director with USP, Alafua Campus in Apia, Sāmoa. He is Sāmoa's foremost choreographer.

father that would accept me, and a mother that would accept me for who I really was. And he did that for me. I think that's my connection to him and I will never forget that.

I'm from Sāmoa originally. I work here in Oceania Centre for Arts, Culture and Pacific Studies – now with Pacific studies. I'm director here for the dance theatre, Oceanic dance theatre, also for choreographing programs here, dances here. I write poetry, I scriptwrite.

I think being interested in the arts was always a passion from when I was a little kid. Growing up in Sāmoa they were having any opportunities to have any kind of free expression, other than traditional dance, of course, when we were in school, primary school to high school. I left to New Zealand in 1989, and then I came back to Sāmoa in 1994, the end of '94 beginning '95.

And during the time in New Zealand I was doing high scores. But most of the time I was doing theatre in downtown Auckland. I've always been interested in dance and theatre. I suppose when you are in theatre or dance you take on a different persona. Going back to Sāmoa after high school I was really torn between modern dance that I was exposed to in New Zealand; [in Sāmoa] they are only for traditional arts and dance, I started to realise after returning.

While I was in Sāmoa, I was working for the National University of Sāmoa and the Marist campus. And there I developed another genre, and that was in the bringing in together tradition and modern dance and theatre. I created a production of *In the Arms of Tagaloa*, which was very successful at the time. It was about New Zealand and finding conflicting cultural conventions or traditions. About the different society that was then the place for a new person or a returning person in Sāmoa. It was very successful in that the videotapes were sold everywhere and duplicated in New Zealand, Australia and America, and in the Sāmoa community. And they were approaching me to do that in their community, the groups in those different communities of Sāmoa.

I got a scholarship to come to Fiji to study expressive arts.

Actually it was to study law here, but I changed that when I came here to expressive arts. And that expressive arts had three strands: dance, music and theatre. But dance was absent – was only on the calendar, wasn't offered. So I created my own dance. At the time, the center had just been established in '97, I came in '98. So I came and saw Epeli and asked him for space to create dance. And since then I started having workshops and just created my own voice really. Expression of what I thought was contemporary Oceania dance. And that is really the freestyle expression of today. Bringing in both elements of tradition and culture. As artists we are given that responsibility. So by using the arts, the dance, the theatre, and music, we weave together all the different things that are actually affecting society at the time.

My teaching philosophy is based on civil motifs. I base it on the creation of the Samoan house or fale. And the Samoan fale is really, well because it's of different arts – the foundation, the pillars, and the ending, which is the taualuga. The foundation is very much the research part. The pillars, I equate it to technique and, of course, what is happening around the social scene – what's happening around in any part of the Pacific. And then the roofing of the house, or the aso of the house, is all the different weavings that are complicated and complex. And that's the site of the feel and the mood and the energy of all of those different things about dance. And of course the last, which is the roof – the taualuga – that would be my juxtaposition of the production, of whatever it is trying to do.

And in this product of dance, the presentation of beats, you can see also the fale is free. The fale doesn't have wings, walls; it's a place for shelter. All the qualities of fale is what I feel about dance. It's open. It's for people to look at and come watch. It's shared. I believe all the things that are happening to us, all the social things, is for us to come together as a community. So in that sense, it is a community engagement and there's a lot to do with banding together to work together in that.

Epeli Hau'ofa – everyone knows him as Epeli because he was very humble – I believe is the greatest man in the whole of the Pacific Oceania because he was a non-conventionalist. He broke every boundary. He basically told everybody that a piece of paper is not really everything, although it's nice to have it. Because he was the father, he nurtured, empowered and inspired so many people, artists and academics alike. He created the Oceania Centre with the intention that it would nurture the spirit of creativity and to draw from traditional motifs and beliefs and values of Pacific Islanders and their cultures and to create something that they can find that is meaningful to their lives today. And I believe this place, Oceania Centre, launched so many people including myself.

Space for true expression, that's what I've always been trying to communicate with everyone. Our everyday life here at the center has always been open and free away from all the discrimination and all of that. I believe when we first came to the center, our artists who were Fijian were a bit reserved when it came to speaking with me, but today are just the most accepting. I think because of our Fijian background, you know, men are taught to be very staunch around females. But because Epeli was so comfortable with being around me and later on all the fa'afafines and the young gauris,[3] so to speak, who are around that make most of the dance theatre core dances. I don't treat men or women differently. I believe that when we're doing work, we focus on the truthfulness of the expression or whatever theme it is you are trying to work on.

Taualuga as I had equated it with the production or presentation of something is very much about the paramountcy of what you're doing and when you're presenting something you are giving it with your mana and you're giving it with love in that you're sharing it with people, hopefully to make a difference and hopefully to make them see another perspective as well. The taualuga in the very traditional sense is very much the end of every piece of entertainment. Now, with that, the taualuga of the fale consolidates … maybe finishes everything and then

---

3   Gauri: Fijian transgender.

it's ready for presentation. And this presentation in my Oceanic dance is the culmination of my philosophy – combination of the experiences in here and wrapping it together in a presentation to hopefully be in some use to whoever is watching.

Change is everywhere. Change is inevitable and change is constant. That's the only thing I believe is constant, is change, you know. We're now being pushed into living in this globalised village, technology is influencing the way people live, influencing lifestyles, ways of thinking, Westernisation, all of that. And now we look around: climate change. And also the way people think of religion as spirituality is not the same as before. So whether that's a good or bad thing it still remains to be debated because there are good sides to change and there are bad sides to change.

When I dance, it is the time for that change. We're no longer living in huts, in falesamoas. We're now living in falepalagis; we have the luxury of DVDs. We are provided by all these different mediums from Western culture, and now we're also creating that too. So change in my dance is that I believe I want it to be inspirational and an empowerment, because it is inevitable.

But my dance does not reproduce what has been done in the traditional sense. My dance, however, draws from those inspirations and aspires to create something new and unique but at the same time carrying the essence of my culture. So whether it's movement, whether it's an issue, whether it's different motifs and all of that, at least it has some of that cultural essence with it, but at the same time evolving, because we are changing. Who knows, ten years from now we'll be thinking differently than how we do now, not losing our values, or not losing our essence as Pacific Islanders. Because that's the only treasure box we can go through to really find our identity and find out who we are. Oh, my treasure box is with me. It's built into my bones and it's running through my veins.

Change is also bringing in so many things right now. It's facilitating our easy access from coming and going and going overseas elsewhere. In half a year, I've been to five different places internationally and within the region. So this whole idea of easy access, of easy movement, has created with it new possibilities for the good or bad. They all, you know, remain to be looked at microscopically. In my relationship, having being in Fiji and going to Sāmoa back and forth has allowed me to be fa`afafine. And having somebody of Futunan descent as my partner, my lover, has actually given me strength in different dimensions in how I see things.

This would never have happened if I was stuck in Sāmoa or living a traditional kind of life, because as you know, Sāmoa has a different take on fa`afafine. Even though it seems to be accepted, underneath the cover it is not. I'm able to connect here at a much deeper level. And also, being able to be accepted by his family, that's warm, that's accepting and loving, which I wouldn't have experienced in Sāmoa. As you know change is also making people take to material things. It's so different in Sāmoa with men. They only want your money.

Well, there's a lot in this interview! I never thought that I'd ever get up there. I never thought I'd get a tattoo – and it's a man's tattoo. However, the song was that the women swam to Sāmoa from Fiji to tattoo the women, not to tattoo the men. But after they dived down for clams, as they were very hungry, they forgot the songs. So they just tattooed the men. And the women were given the smaller tattoo. My tattoo has always been very special to me because my father was never accepting of me as a fa`afafine before. And when he asked me to get a tattoo, if I was game enough for a tattoo, I was thinking, Okay, this is your last challenge, to try to conform me and make me a man. I said, Okay, bring it on. And I got tattooed only like five days and luckily I got a booking. But I think it made my father – it created a connection that was deeper, for my father and me, and it also reconciled a lot of my differences. Before we never saw eye to eye. And after the tattoo, it served as a reconciliation mechanism.

Go with my mana.
Mana is more than power. Mana is more than essence as well.
Mana is my connections and that's not just physical or mental
or emotional but spiritual as well. So my mana is … When I
say go with my mana, it will assist you in whatever you do.

Resitara Apa
Photograph: Courtesy of contributor

Resitara Apa

I'm from the villages of Moata`a and Safune in Savai`i. I was the acting CEO for the Sāmoa AIDS Foundation and the secretariat coordinator for the Pacific Sexual Diversity Network.

For me growing up as a fa`afafine, I can relay being at a very young age as a fa`afafine, say at seven or six, that's when I knew because I was always playing with my sisters' dolls and wanting that sort of stuff. At that age I had big feet and I still have very big feet at the moment and my sisters used to make me break in their shoes so I'd run around the house this little young boy wearing high heels. And my parents they didn't mind. I think they sort of knew at that very young age for me being a fa`afafine.

There was still a stigma and discrimination coming from my extended family. Being that my father was in a high-profile position, he was ambassador for Sāmoa to New Zealand, and they sort of had this image of how that family should be and there was still a lot of that coming through and most of my extended family were all from the new churches so they had their own way of approaching what I should become. But for me at that age I knew, myself, as long as my parents and my siblings accepted me for who I am I'm fine, I don't need to prove myself to anyone else, as long as these people are happy I'm happy. Coming through life I never had to come out to my parents and family. They accepted and saw me for who I was when I was young and becoming the person I am today. There was no need for me to go, 'Mum, Dad, I am fa`afafine.' Instead, I said to them, 'Mum, Dad, this is who I am.'

It's been a beautiful ride for me with my family. If there was anything I would change – there is nothing – these are the people who has supported me through life and being there for me for everything. We do have our ups and downs at home but it's normal amongst siblings. But my parents have been the most supportive people I've known. I remember my mum she used to beat me up, you know the Samoan mother with jandals and salu lima and beat you up and say, 'Ke fia keige a e ete le iloa fai feau fa`a teine!' Meaning, 'You want be a woman yet you do not how to do woman's chores!'

For me at that time I didn't take it seriously, thinking, 'Oh yeah blah, blah, blah ...' But now I can see where they were coming from – they weren't pushing for me to become this person but they were sort of supporting me and it's their way of acceptance for me.

I remember at one stage when I was in church in Sāmoa at the age of twelve, at church on father's day and, you know, in Sāmoa father's day is a big thing back then ... So the faife`au for his last service in the evening he was going on about Gomorrah and Sodom and he was going on and on about that, you know, gay lifestyle this and that. So everybody left the church and it was just me and my father walking hand in hand going back home and you know – for it was quite amazing at the time and still is – because my father grabbed my hand as we were walking home and he turned to me and said, 'Son, do you understand what the priest was going on about? Are you okay?' And I said 'Yeah I'm fine,' and he turned to me and he goes, 'No matter what path you take in life be assured that we are right behind you and support you.'

This is coming to someone that's twelve years old. It's always stayed with me throughout the rest of my life that – him accepting me at that young age, not knowing, him sensing that this is who I was going to be.

It's been a blessing being brought up with this family compared to seeing other fa`afafines in their families who struggle, being beaten up and being outcasted and thrown out from their families. I wonder how they feel because I really can't say I know what they are going through. I say I was given the silver spoon, this family has been so supportive, they come and watch my shows and my mum she is a strong supporter of my shows and my father he wants to get me drunk before I do my shows, bless his soul, he passed away … but that's how I've become who I am. I've gained my strength and am comfortable in being who I am because it comes from them, and if it wasn't for them I don't know what I would be doing.

I was in girl's clothes back then during the daytime but even though I don't have the boobs I still consider myself a fa`afafine because that's what my identity is to being Samoan is a fa`afafine. I can't go to Tonga and say I'm a fakaleiti,[1] no. Whatever country I go to I say I'm a fa`afafine. At the opening of a diplomatic consultation I just came back from I said, 'Us from the Pacific we do not adopt to SMS or LGBT or whatever name you may call us because we are known through our cultural terms like fa`afafine, fakaleiti, vakasalewalewa,[2] that's who we are. We are not drag queens, or female impersonators trying to impersonate somebody, no. We are who we are.'

I have some people approach me – like this guy from New Zealand, he goes around the Pacific, Roland or something – and we did an interview and he kept asking me four times, 'Is it true that if you were born from a family of so many boys you were chosen to be fa`afafine?' and I said, 'No it is not true, we are born who we are. I know families where all the brothers are fa`afafine and I know families who have fa`afafine and fa`atama in their family, so it's not true.' But I knew that he was trying to get me to say 'yes it's true' but I can't say yes to something it is not true because I know it's not true because we are born this way, this is who we are.

Along my travels to being who I am has been a lot of fun and it's been a wonderful trip, bumpy most of the times, a rollercoaster ride but, you know, I've met a lot of interesting people trying to make who I am. Going to school I used to be

---

1 Fakaleiti: Tongan transgender.
2 Vakasalewalewa: Fijian transgender.

bullied and most fa`afafine were bullied and we Samoans, we have a pride in ourselves which we cannot go running home and going 'Mummy that boy was beating me up.' No, we don't do that – we end up confronting them ourselves and those little things in life has made me stronger and I'm ready to go out there and be who I am.

I remember incidents at school where I was in the bathroom, next minute a bucket of water comes raining down on me and some of the other fa`afafine girls would be drenched wet – those sorts of incidents, and name-callings. I remember when you were called a fa`afafine – this is going back twenty, thirty years – if you were called a fa`afafine you were like, 'I'm not a fa`afafine!' it felt like an insult back then, you with the word fa`afafine itself. But now it's commonly used, everybody's woken up to it ... But being name-called ... And most fa`afafines had a fear of playing sports because it was either the girls play netball or the boys play rugby, one or the other, that was it – we had fa`afafines coming to school with medical certificates just to avoid that day of playing games.

It was a lot of name-calling for me – it wasn't much of the physical side, it was more of the mental side with the name-calling and harassment. And there was nobody to turn to and although my family was appreciative of me I felt like I didn't want to put a burden on them. I dealt with it by trying to be strong. I said to myself, 'This is who I am. What they are calling me, I gonna prove them wrong by ensuring that I'm excelling well in school' – and I did. That was my fight: it was like, 'You call me names? You push me towards being a better person.'

If I went to my parents and tell them what's happening in school, it's all because of who I am – the blame would end up being on me. It would be like, see what happens if you end up being me. I had that fear at the back of my head, like they might blame me for being who I am – that's why all this negativity is coming from everybody. All fa`afafines I do know, all handled it themselves. Some of them I do know they have fistfights and some of them verbally attack back.

The current climate on homophobia in Sāmoa is very strong there; it's still there in Sāmoa. Just for example us walking up the stairs now, it's just those little name-calling and repeating how we speak and so forth. It's homophobia in a form of verbal abuse but not physical abuse – it's more on the mental side. Like when you go to clubs … People ask, 'Why aren't there any gay clubs in Sāmoa?' I'm like 'Why do we need gay clubs in Sāmoa?' People understand who we are in these clubs …

But the introduction of new religious churches – they are the ones enforcing and waking up the homophobia again, feeding people with the mindframe of 'it's a sin', and yet people will eventually hate the person for who they are. Sometime I say, 'don't hate the sinner, hate the sin' because they are not the one doing that … But there is a very strong homophobia still in Sāmoa, I can see it in the schools. Most of the faʻafafines are dropping out of school because they can't tolerate the stigma and discrimination that's going on.

They are turning to the avenue of streetwork and moving away from families, being with other queens who are not employed and don't have the resources for them to move on. So it's a very dangerous lifestyle because most of these queens end up having random sex everywhere and it adds to high profiles of STIs and HIVs, which is where I'm advocating they protect themselves. They are moving out of school at such a young age without knowledge. Some of them still can't understand English and some of them can't read. Those are things that link up to homophobia because these poor girls leave school just to run away from it because there is no counselling, there is no mentoring for these girls.

Faʻafatama is very underground. How shall I put it? It's like taboo, actually taboo for some. We do see lesbians now and then on the road but there are not … but people can't see them as a couple, they call them a tomboy, linking them to a man … But there are some I know of that do have female partners, and people don't talk about it. I know some high-profile people who have partners and people don't talk about it, it's just not to be talked about it. It's the taboo that's there, you know, leave it as it is, don't wake it up.

Fa'afafine on the other case, because we are everywhere, colorful, don't give a crap about people now, that's why the focus is more on fa'afafine because they are visible. We have been called the cause of HIV and STI in Sāmoa and it's just because people have no knowledge or little knowledge of these diseases and viruses as well as of contracting them ... There still is a lot of work that needs to be done in getting people's behaviour to change towards fa'afafine.

Fa'afafine, we know our boundaries when it comes to that. I know my sister, I know my girls. Even I remember an incident where a well-known fa'afafine, she's in New Zealand now, she beat up a girl at one of the clubs, and all the fa'afafines here were outraged. Why? You know, you never touch a girl, as the Bible says, the girl is an apple of a brother's eye. We may dress we may act we may feel as a woman but we do know our cultural boundaries. The women are sacred to us – even though we might have the chop and have boobs and do that ... I will still know who I am as a fa'afafine, and I consider myself as a fa'afafine not a woman ...

There is lot that needs to change. We have to start from the top, from the village leaders, community leaders, the churches as well – they play a vital part in Samoan history and people have adapted church and culture together, so culture now, everything now is offered to the churches or given to the churches. And for the health sector and the Sāmoa Fa'afafine Association and myself to work with the churches to ensure that everybody is living a life that they should live, a life of freedom without discrimination, a life of happiness and a life of fulfillment.

Those are the key people that you need to approach, especially for Sāmoa: the religious leaders and community leaders, starting from the village council and the government – they are the ones that can push it, they are the ones that has the money for it to happen.

Growing up in Remuera, back in Auckland in the seventies

with my siblings – this was when my dad was an ambassador for New Zealand – they could see that I was who I was, you know, and I could still feel that some were put off because of me being at that young age identifying who I was. My siblings and I have a beautiful relationship back when I was very young. My sister I'm staying with now, she's the one that understands who I am – and they call me always Tara.

I can sense in their eyes that it was difficult for them because there were only two of us boys that's trying to continue on the family name, that type of thing, but it became a full stop for me … But for them, I think that was the fear they had – I could see that – 'Oh my gosh, you know what's gonna happen now?' But the achievements that I've done, I've gained their respect from that.

Coming up in that surrounding, as I've said before, living in that environment of happiness, of nobody trying to push me or mould me into something that I wasn't, was very enriching for me. That's why I said before, it's really difficult for me to understand the struggles and the pains that other girls go through because I sit back and I'm like, 'You poor thing, I wonder how that felt?' I really can't relate to that.

My siblings have always been supportive of me, like, sometimes … like now, my sister in Australia she sends me a wig, my mum she sends me box of panties – that sort of things. They buy me those little girlie stuff. It's quite amazing because I've sort of moved from wearing girlie stuff – only for my shows now – but they are still doing it! And I can't tell them I don't want them anymore and it will be like I've changed my mind again … But I'm comfortable with who I am now, I've already found out who I am … But it's the thought that counts: if they bring it, I still keep it and I won't return them back … No I won't wear it … it's the thought that counts.

You know, for me, I'm not trying to turn away from being, you know … I have painted fingernails, plucked eyebrows, my long hair, I'm like a tomboy with my shaven legs … Do you wanna see my Brazilian?! Hahahaha!! Call me a tomboy, you know, that sort of thing – because at night Taira does come out with a vengeance that's when you see Taira out at night it's because I'm comfortable. People say, 'Why don't you dress up like that during the daytime?' I'm like, at night time it takes more effort for me to look that glamorous, you know? As, if I was running around the whole day looking like that by the end of the day I would probably look like something out of 'zombies hit Sāmoa' or something like that! You know it might have my eyeliner down to my cheeks, it might end up like that! I'm just comfortable for who I am, you know, and sometimes I don't feel like it.

The consultation I went to in Brazil, I showed them my photos of my being in drag and they said, 'Why don't you dress up like that here?' And I'm like, I'm comfortable like this, you know, and that's the perception people have, you know, why don't you dress up like that in the daytime and night-time? but I'm comfortable with it, you know. You can think otherwise, but this is me.

Everyone has their hero. My father was my hero. In looking back when I was young … for a Samoan man … When I was seven, eight, we used to live in this three-story mansion in Remuera, you know big house, we had two maids and a butler and so forth … The minute I know it's five o'clock in the afternoon, and at fifteen minutes past five I hear the front door close, I would go and hide. We had this game of hide and seek, we played it every day after work, and he would come and look for me. And he was my hero like that. I don't know if Samoan fathers do that now because the only reason you would go and hide is because he is going to beat you up, hahaha! But me and my dad we had a hide and seek game going on and that was our relationship, that was our friend. It was like a very modernised, Westernised Samoan family that was loving and caring.

I had a weird childhood because the thing was – it's gonna sound scary now for you guys – but we used to have dolls and I used to put them on fire and throw them in the closet at home. These dolls and teddy bears, I would lock myself up in the closet and play with a doll, that's probably what the term coming out of the closet means, but I used to light the dolls on fire and throw them into the closet. But that's what I used to love doing when I was young. I remember we had a cocktail party at home and all the firemen came in and at that young age I was busy eyeing up the firemen. It's just these little things in life that I went through. Why would I light the dolls? I'm still trying to see why, I had this fascination with fire, I needed to play with fire, to burn things, to burn dolls, and it's a weird sensation for me – and as a fa`afafine it's really weird.

In New Zealand and Australia I had to adapt to that Western life: I couldn't be the fa`afafine I had to be. I had to go and cut my hair, wear a suit, wear a tie to get a good job, and I couldn't express who I was and from keeping all of that in me, you know? Oh, it was frustration … [so] that when I came back here, I finally realised I can be myself back here, without the name-calling talking, without stares, without looks from people; as for New Zealand and Australia, the minute you leave Oxford Street and you're on that train to Mount Dewitt, gosh! You are stared at, you are name-called at, probably get beaten up before you get home.

It's funny how I left Sāmoa when I – at a young age – I left Sāmoa to go to Australia … I left Sāmoa to get away from the Samoan stuff, the culture … I left Sāmoa to go to New Zealand, saw the bright lights and I had a good job but I would go into prostitution, you know how Samoan queens get drunk, we go to a social, 'Tatou o, kuku i le sukuliki, let's go on the street,' just to get a quick fuck, but after a while prostitution took over.

I left my job and I became a prostitute … You know, the sex wasn't fun anymore it was just like money, money, money. So after coming first at Miss Le Penina [beauty pageant] in 1997, I decided this is eating me up here, doing this kind of work I'm not getting any motivation, so I moved to Australia to run away from prostitution. So I run away to Australia – wonderful job, wonderful everything – but the drugs kicks in. So the drugs scene kicks in and I'm taking drugs; spending 700 a weekend just Saturdays and Sundays on coke, speed, whatever, you name it. On the top of that another 500 on alcohol; and this is like every weekend. Those sort of things I saw …

It was actually Mum that put me back into place just by asking me simple questions like, 'How are you? Have you seen your family back home?' and I realised my family is here to stay, you know. And drugs were not doing me any good, it was eating up my life and spending a lot on it, so I thought, 'Okay, it's time for me to move back home.'

But then my relationship with my father grew stronger through moving back here to Sāmoa, when Dad was Secretary for Justice and Mum was the secretary for the police commissioner; and for me I took that as pride and I wanted to make them happy. So I took my father's – you know, the way he was and the way he was respected – and I saw that if he is respected like that in the community and in the country, I had to get that respect back, and I had to earn that respect too – and to know who I am. Dad did it in a very academic setting, but I did it in the entertainment and the advocacy. I am reflecting my father, I am reflecting his footsteps, and Mum – even couple of days ago after returning back from Brazil – she reflected on it by saying, 'Your father, those are the places your father went to, India, Brazil, Argentina for United Nations trips,' and I went through UNESCO, so gosh, I'm actually following in his footsteps.

I felt like I had not followed in his footsteps, I felt like I had not accomplished where he got to, saying goodbye to him at his funeral. Everybody just stood back and everybody saying goodbye to him at his coffin. I said to him, you know, in Samoan I said to him, 'I'm so sorry, Dad, I couldn't be the son who you wanted me to be,' and everybody started bursting out into tears, but for me … I felt I had let him down with that.

But Mum came up to me right after we buried Dad and she goes, 'Your father was proud of you, your father was happy that you became who you are without us tell you somebody you weren't.' It was like it had come full circle.

My relationship with my mum is a beautiful relationship. I would say she is the person that has moulded me to be somebody strong. She has given me the strength to move on to the next day, to ensure I don't do loans, somebody that doesn't rely on other people for things, rely on other people for comfort and love and friendship, don't rely on people for material things – that's what my mother has given me. She has given me the sense of belonging, given me the sense of family, to ensure that I connect with my family. I felt like I have come back home, and my mum was here, my dad was here, and just to finally see them, and I felt appreciated again, felt comforted and loved. I can be humble and I can be crazy, and I can be the best of both worlds, like now. I am a woman and I can do 110% of what a woman does and 150% of what a man does.

And now I'm advocating for fa`afafines. When I was in New Zealand, well – I'm going to take you right back to where I started. After a friend's funeral, that sort of kicked in because HIV and AIDS were new for me, it took me to thinking a lot of my friends are starting to die from this illness. At the time I was still working in hospitality and everywhere I went I would apply as a waiter but they would give me the manager's job. I always like to start from the bottom and make my way up but they like to give me the manager's job ... So I was at the management level but when I came back to Sāmoa I was approached by Jay and Tasi to come and manage Paddles and I took that job up, and at the same time I had made good friends with Ken Moala, bless his soul, is he still alive? hahaha! He's going to kill me ... anyway Ken started the Sāmoa AIDS Foundation. So you – us – fa`afafines, we are naturally talented in the arts and performance and whatever, you're new at it, we are talented at it. So he approached me and asked me to take over.

So I did take over for a while, and while I was doing that I was still going back to school doing administration, business management, that sort of stuff at USP.[3] As I was doing that I identified that my area was actually advocating, going out to international funders and donors and conferences and stuff and advocating for Samoan rights, you know, with fa`afafine issues, ensuring that we are heard in the international arena ...

---

3   University of the South Pacific, Alafua Campus, Apia, Sāmoa.

Because most of the time the Pacific is not seen in this arena, it's always been the case that the Pacific issues are never spoken of. I realised that when people say 'Pacific' in these international gatherings, they go, 'Oh, Australia and New Zealand?' That's the Pacific they know, they don't know of the tropical countries; and for me to identify that need ... Ken moulded me to be the person in the leadership role.

I'm happy with what I'm doing at the moment. I see myself holding down this job for another five years, which is the Pacific Sexual Diversity Network – that's the organisation that advocates for fa`afafine issues but also for the Sāmoa AIDS Foundation, because it's taking care of my community, to ensure that my community is well looked after, well informed on HIV and AIDS issues, you know ... Because Sāmoa only has twenty-two cases, but the prevalence of sexually transmitted Infections is phenomenal.

Sāmoa has the highest rates of chlamydia and gonorrhea across the Pacific. Yes, it's something to be ashamed of. It's the Samoan women who are pregnant going to the hospital and getting checked and are found with that. And what my worry is, if there is an alarming rate of STIs recorded, I'm wondering how many cases of HIV and AIDS there are wandering around Sāmoa, because these figures are from last year or two years ago.

People are trusting the system. It's not the confidentiality side, or the anonymous side, it's more getting the people to change their behaviour, change their way of thinking, because now people are still going, 'I don't get that disease; she gets that disease' – they're still pointing the finger, you know, they're still going, 'It's the fa`afafines the ones, with the virus carriers.' It's trying to get people to change their behaviour and their way of thinking. But all the reported cases are heterosexual cases – there has never been a fa`afafine reported case; the only fa`afafine reported cases are from overseas and they are not documented here for Sāmoa. I would say for sexual practises of fa`afafines: it is a very high risk because most do not wear condoms. And most of these practises are around and amongst alcohol. The alcohol is the fusion for the sexual attraction and moving and walking to the seawall and going for it.

Some of the guys like the penetration themselves, the fa`afafine giving them the penetration, and it's vice versa. I'm seeing the young ones who are enjoying it too and they are starting to find pleasure in it. That's my worry because these men, they are having sex with the fa`afafines, they are having sex with women, who knows, they might be having sex with other men, but for fa`afafines it's only straight men, it's only men they know they are straight.

So these are the carriers that are going around, and that I'm worried about at the moment. The reported fa`afafines from overseas, and most of the cases that are brought into Sāmoa, is because it's always the husband who had traveled overseas and come back – so all of the cases that have been reported are all heterosexual.

My advice for fa`afafine is don't be afraid of who you are, embrace your culture, embrace your family, embrace the respect of the people you get. Don't misuse the respect you get; rather, use it in the way that you'll be loved. Sometimes we tend to lose the whole picture once we find the respect from the community or the family. I've seen that once they get respect from the family, that's it, they start bringing boys home, and thinking that they are the Queen B of the family. What I mean is, know how to respect, stay who you are, and love yourself. There is no need to fight amongst ourselves, there is a bigger fight out there that we need to look towards, from bullying to HIV issues. Our identity is very crucial.

Don't be afraid in exploring your horizons. As fa`afafine we can accomplish everything if we put our mind to it, if we have the support. If you get the respect, if you get the support, then you will be able to move on.

After travelling around the world, people ask me and I say, 'I'm fa`afafine' and they say 'You're what?' and I say, 'This is what a fa`afafine is'.

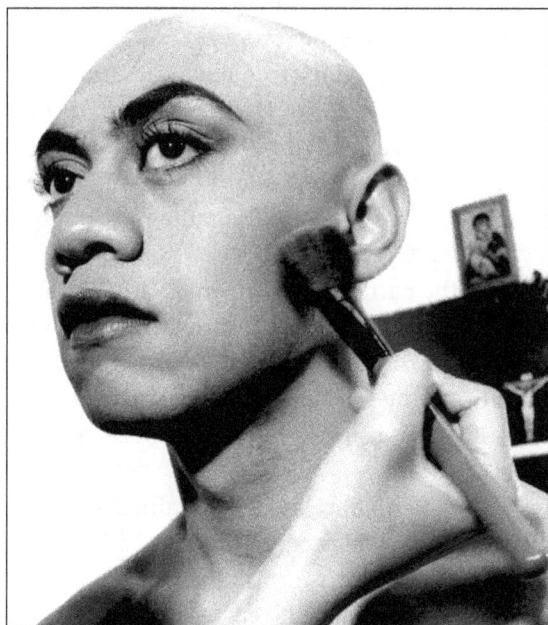

Brian Fuata
Photographer: Heidrun Lohr, 2003,
The Performance Space, Sydney

Brian Fuata

FA`AFAFINE[1]

1. COMMANDMENTS *(voiceover)*
My mother was very superstitious.
Most of her superstitions, oddly enough, had a specific time:
Midnight and any time after midnight but before sunrise …

1. Never look into a mirror.
2. Never whistle.
3. Never be awake with a window opened.
4. At all times, day and night, avoid contact with an Aiku — an evil male demon that sits in trees, waiting for girls, waiting to jump into them and possess them, because they are jealous of the girls' long hair.
5. Clear stockings are to be worn at all times on Sundays.
6. A lady never talks with a member of the opposite sex without her guardian.
7. Never kiss on the lips in public toilets.
8. Your name is 'Gary Cooper', and you have never been with a guy before.
9. Never seduce your mother.
10. Always love someone who can never love in return.
11. Never answer a slow tapping or scratching at the door.
12. Never approach – and avoid at all times – roaming dogs or cats.
13. Never fall in love with your children.

---

1 Fa`afafine is a performance piece by Brian Fuata, which was commissioned by Urban Theatre Projects, Bankstown, in Sydney, Australia. Directed by Nigel Kellaway, with dramaturgy by Damien Millar, produced by Harley Stumm.

2. BIRTH

There's something happening that no one else is quite sure of, but you and I have known exists somewhere out near the borders of foreign countries, where passers by acknowledge each other with side glances and weird white science.

Goodbye to mothers.

I gave birth to mine on the 26th of July 1978 in Wellington hospital, Wellington, N.Z.

The nine months leading to her departure were fair sailing …

And I hadn't much difficulty understanding the miracle happening inside me.

I had eaten well, exercised regularly, went to my breathing classes, took up yoga, gave up cigarettes and alcohol and acquired three substantial relationships with three smart, handsome, intelligent and very well endowed men. Who supported me greatly during the ten minutes of my labour.

It took less than five pushes and not much breathing when my mother slid out and severed a farewell. It has devastated me ever since.

I'll have lost her several times over, and it will devastate me even more to the point where I'll have given birth to many more mothers in retribution to the many I have lost to hysteria, to utopia, to gossip, to free drugs and public toilets, to anonymity – and his many fears towards intimacy.

(Hula)

3. AND THEN THERE IS ME AND MY MUM

Tonight I will crisscross this city's spine and bark wanting something more. There will be no apology, tonight …

There's this cute boy on the train who looks like Gary Cooper travelling backwards reading maps and desiring vacant lots of casual sex. Last night I fucked him.

Sorry. I'll say something pretty.

My mother is feeling maybe she should start writing letters to Gary Cooper since he's never home to answer the telephone –

(Drunk) 'Mr. Cooper, please call immediately … Hey Mister Cooper, I have lost the word and can't remember a single gesture.'

No Mum, there will be no applauding from the crowd tonight. You have lost your rule.

But Brian is doing very well. He's moved down to Sydney and is living with two females.

Mum, I like dresses. I like mohawks. And I like being a boy. Mum is happy.

When I was eight, I told her that I found Jesus attractive. She hit me, sent me to my bedroom, and closed the door. Not long after she came running in to pull the bed sheets off me, and accused me of being naughty. A few months later she repapered the living room with a huge image of Jesus. I liked it.

(High-heel shoes on)

When I was eighteen, I moved to Sydney. She called twice a day without fail for a week, saying nothing but crying, sometimes really hysterically, other times just sobs and sniffles. I just listened through the five minutes and then I'd hang up.

I wanted her to ask me to forgive her. I wanted to remind her that I was NOT a fa`afafine.

4.   CHAT SHOW

HOSTESS: Good evening!!! Tonight we're asking who does what, to whom, who likes what, who likes doing what, and what and to whom.

Brian, do you recognise this voice?

MUM *(voiceover – drunk)*: Where there is a boy there is method.

And if you want to wear a frock, Brian, you can wash the fucking dishes.

Where there is method there is a mother.

There are other reasons to wear a frock!

1. Does a fa`afafine need to wear a dress?
    No!!!!!!
    Have you any idea what FA`AFAFINE means…literally?!

It means 'LIKE A WOMAN'.
Does that mean that every drag queen in Sāmoa is a fa`afafine?
Confused?
I think I'd better take your boyfriend!

2. *(Take boyfriend to seats)*
Don't worry, not every fa`afafine is gay

3. *(Moving back to tables)*
Can anyone tell me the fa`afafine's favourite color?
I'll tell you later.

4. Are Samoan mother's comfortable with gay men?
Usually not
Are there any gay men here this evening?
You'd better all come with me!

5. *(All gay men to the seats)*
Are the men who fuck fa`afafine gay?
Not necessarily
Or so they claim ... do they do it in the dark?!

6. Can a fa`afafine marry a nice girl and have children?
Yes!
Who creates a fa`afafine – men or women?
Women – their mothers.
Come on boys, we're not safe here – all of you up here

(All men to seats)

'I have cleaned the house several times but all with different intentions, some not all that clean. Mopping the floor, washing and drying the dishes, wrung many clothes on the line surrounded by a taro garden that takes up the entire backyard.'

Samoan families can be very big – you pray for daughters – but if not ...

(Scrim lowers)

I am a White Fucker.

Fucking white men has never been an 'option', but a cultural imperative. It is for the benefit of anthropology. I have been known to have a relationship with colored boys, all of whom have been as interesting and developed as some East African countries. The one colored boy in particular (who was the most developed) was my cousin who everyone called 'MacGyver', for no reason. (Samoans don't have reason, we ate it).

I remember him sucking me off and nothing happening.

He would cordon off the back of his throat, collect so much saliva, which poured into my mouth as if he was watering me.

I began to learn about the human boy. My education with MacGyver instructed a sweet perversity in retrospect, but I have never forgotten that naked boys in beds know absolutely nothing, but sensations and darkness.

But with color, as in a darker pigmentation of the skin, MacGyver taught me nothing about the color of mine; until I watched TV and got sexual crushes (which meant rubbing the corner of pillows between my legs) on all these white men parading in American soaps.

So, White fucking it is.

Over the years I have learnt to love being a White Fucker. I hate them.

Without you I would feel a great loss of identity.

5. TABLE

My mother and all her friends meet up at each other's house to play poker without sleep, laughing and singing till Kingdom come. Literally spending twenty-four hours smoking cartons of cigarettes, drinking bourbons and coke, gambling half their week's earnings to pay respect to their idol and their idiot, the Virgin Mother Mary. Thinking how stupid that some nigger could have such a high demanding job and still not have anything to show for it. Because as far as they are concerned Mary is no different from Tina Mulipu who works at the shoe store her Palagi husband owns. At least Tina gets discount shoes.

Meanwhile us children wait in the peripheries anticipating the odd note or coin to fall off the table and into our pockets, I being the little girl that I am have the advantage of being allowed to sit underneath the table, and under there I sit. Sexy platform-shoes. In the wrong hands one too easily falls over into a coma of marriage to the local pharmacist, who calls all you islander women 'Blossom', and later shortens it to 'Loss'.

PHARMACIST *(voiceover)*: Come here my beautiful Loss, I haven't seen you for a while.

Come marry me, my one and only Loss, we've nothing to lose.

Surrounded by a sea of legs, brown legs, women's legs, mothers legs saturated in cheap perfume, baby oil and the cynicism that Jesus was like any other sailor they had met in the early seventies.

Back then, you women was Sex in platform shoes — both functional and naïve; sexy platform shoes and a sea of legs.

And above this water's line a collective of strangers sound their laughter like puberty, and in this little girl that I'm not, a drunk-yard of happy women, where down and down I sink.

The foreskin has medicinal properties. You softly rub mine on your sick eye while I stupidly argue with the girls in the family over how I can't see the television – 'Because you're in my way!' And after a few minutes your eye becomes soothed and James, my older brother, is thankful that he doesn't have to do it this time.

Tonight, underneath, I am sitting on a woman's big toe and my arsehole is safe and secure ... With your tears wept on the tip of my groin, I fumble my underwear back on and continue watching the television, now made clear and in full view.

And sucking on a hard-boiled sweet I realise I am facing right in between my mother's legs where I continue sucking. Her thighs are two whales, thick and blubber, sweating concern for her children's ability to walk well into the future and I all of a sudden run dry in the mouth. I am strangely intrigued, waiting for something to come gushing out from between her legs, but nothing does, so I will wait a little longer.

6. FIRST GOSPEL, ACCORDING TO THE MOTHER

Her hand on my mother's thigh smelt like God where salt burnt my skin and Sodom and Gomorrah! I couldn't breathe. My mother's legs opened further apart where above this water's line I could hear their laughter sing like memory where down, down I sank drowning in this sea of legs, brown legs, women's legs, mothers' legs, and my dick pissed my pants and I realised I was a ... and Sodom and Gomorrah! I couldn't, I couldn't breathe ...

Her hand went further up my mother's legs, the liquid that ran down mine became thick like paste and stuck my legs together and I couldn't, fucken, breathe ... saturated in cheap perfume, baby oil and the cynicism that Jesus was just like any other sailor they had met, I tried ... nothing came out but kissing sounds and the fuck of my cold body flip flapping on the suburban ocean floor. My toes disappeared, my ankles became one, the salt that I perspired became crusted, flaking away to reveal silver specks of scales. My mother was happiness ... 'Brian's doing well, he's moved down to Sydney and living with two females!' ...

And after swimming around these strangers' legs, I swam out from underneath the table and into the midnight streets, realising, for the first time, I can never have what these women had.

And she would genuflect her stupid knee, sit her arse on the floor, cross her legs like Buddha — 'What more can you do to please me?' — and I would position my groin like lamb on marble and she would receive ... into her eye ... Jesus.

And then, in 1987, my mother was possessed...

By her dead sister...

7.–8. THE EXORCIST – PART 1

Okay, so there's this Samoan family in the lounge room reciting the usual evening prayer.

Not long after we finish, my mother starts rolling her head in circles and her arms and hands rotate like a chopper.

She yells at the children, 'You're ugly and disrespectful and where the fuck are my kids!' Pointing at me, 'Who are you?

I know you, you're trouble and your mother's going to pay for it.'
The others run to their rooms. I follow.

(Run back to get radio microphone)

So my mother was possessed,
Maybe by Auntie Maria,
And she is vomiting shit and silly regrets of leaving her children in rotting families,
'You're dad's responsible.'
My mother is not my mother
And my dad's scared.
He's shaking his head thinking 'not again.'
He hated Auntie Maria.
Screams and screaming and panties drenched in piss, and her face is pleasantly sour, and there are contortions and yellow eyes and bibles flipping like a multitude of fish gasping for a multitude of loaves, and my living aunties show up.
My dad doesn't like them either.
They've got this white priest man,
That all the parishioners have crushes on 'cause he was sex.
'Fr Frank, you fucken slut! Are you going to fuck me too?!!'
'Cause he was just sex ...

PRIEST: *In the beginning was the word, and the word was God.*
And cultural catamites that refuse to mention names, professions and familial beliefs for fear their girlfriends or possible girlfriends would turn into stone and die in shit, loiter in church pews reciting creeds to affirm family ties and strengthen the voices of the parish choir. Cautious that no note is overlooked and the cocks of the men in mass remain moist.
BRIAN: And we children are scared, and we're called upon to witness a sacred Samoan custom, where the living aunties are standing on my mother who is not my mother and beating her body to get to Maria.
And Dad's rolling his eyes.
There's something happening that no one else has caught on

to and you are relishing the glory of others not knowing. Your children are reading and speaking in fluent English. They are far more articulate than the average 'child' and seem to be a lot lighter in shade. Almost translucent. Radiant. Closer to God.

And she's bleeding and she's bruised, and they're beating and bruising, and the husband is very proud, as he staunches up and down the isle like Paul Keating[2] and dismisses his people with slight glances like middle class. It is a proud moment for you when your children are the talk of the congregation. Where one of your daughters is a slut with the 'Western morals of a black alley cat!' and she is pretty like ludicrous, like a brochure of your island home, so pretty it's sacrilege.

Your eldest son is visiting home from the army,

Studying microelectronics part-time at university.

Another daughter, the eldest ... although ugly as black-sinned skin, is reading the gospel this morning and reading so well you can see right through her, her bitch black bucked teeth frothing language that your people say 'yes' to, 'thank you', 'what would you like?', 'if you like', 'when you like', nod subserviently, smile unknowingly and end dancing lovely.

Your youngest daughter is doing contemporary liturgical movements that oohs and aahs the parish priest which then oohs and aahhs the parish present left pondering as to where to enrol their brown daughters to follow footsteps of such praise.

9.   BEAT SEX

And then, there is me. And tonight I met a Sex. And it was dead.

Tonight I met him over the phone. And he was dying.

He was effeminately cold and anonymous with the name 'Bob', and he was weathered and withering with disease and we didn't say much – small talk about discount prices, local charges, how monthly payments worked out a lot more cheaper in the long run. And I didn't. And I wasn't. Attracted to him. Most precious of all was my embarrassment.

---

2 Australian Prime Minister 1991–96.

I was embarrassed by the sight of her. After school when she picked me up in front of other students, or on weekends when making that all-important trip, with all my cool friends, trying to avoid her by sitting in another train carriage. Pretending not to hear her when she spoke to me. But she talks forever and she looks ugly.

His lips were independent to the rest of his face, the rest just hung like meat in a sauna. Body was sickly thin and haggard. Skin decorated with lesions. Sweet.

But I wasn't going to cry now, now that she had come all this way in her obviously newly purchased car (she got rid of the old one, it won her no friends). And we went back home and met her maternity. I obliged our stupid contract but suddenly I fell in love.

It was the best Sex I had ever met. But still, I fell in love. I had known of him, and of it and knew them now. I knew his lesions like my childhood. And he knew my childhood better than me. He knew I didn't know anything, that to me, 'Sāmoa' and 'Samoan' were nouns and adjectives — nothing more.

While my fingers were circling his arse I was the prodigal son realising upon a white male pattern. I had heard of it and knew it now. Patterned into a history of sad beautiful neutral cock-moments — for the first time I felt honestly Samoan. A proper one, with a wife, several hundred babies, a job as a factory hand, Catholic with Mormon tendencies, a house, and two cars. Two holy, genuine, newly purchased, family carrying, law abiding, beautiful, natural, moving cars ... Goodbye to mothers.

This is a sign that what we have physically shared has been but a moment, last night, when Christ was washing your feet (you can barely walk these days). This is a moment in time, frozen for you, extended. It is taken for granted that what we have just done could be considered by many a personal cultural trait.

I love you and like all lonely animals in the kingdom I am eternally sorry for your outgoing calls to the bank, to the nursing home where you work inside and in your insides (dealings with old people are hard for you, I know that, we all know that). For the many nights of Bingo with money lost to Tina, Paulita who had just moved from Auckland, Ese`ese who you owe twenty dollars, Bessy and her thirty-year-old manic depressive daughter Rusty, Sau and Eterine. Remember that time when you likened my tummy to licking? We were both very upset.

The absence we have shared has not brought an answer any closer to us. There is a principle, common to the people, that to feel something, it has to be lost. So, goodbye. There was always no belonging, no connected bits or bitings, so goodbye to the tooth that has fallen out, the eye that loves sweet things, and goodbye to you.

10. THE EXORCIST – PART 2
Hi, my name's Brian,

And it's early morning, cold, and we're all trying to sleep in the lounge room. Mum's bleeding and bruised.

'Stop it' she screams. 'Please stop it.' Dad's rolling his eyes. I with all the luck in the world have been chosen to sleep closest to her –

'I'm gonna eat your fucken toes you lil' cunts!' – and the blankets rise to our knees revealing our feet while we writhe like sleeping misfits, because our mother has evil in her, and Auntie Maria. And boogies have always existed, in the cupboard, and under our beds, fucking rosary beads then spitting them out like pips.

And we're exhausted from the night's exorcism and don't go to sleep, but pretend to.

There's a scratching at the door and I know it's the possessed cat we were all told about in Sunday school, or maybe it's Mum, and it's wanting to possess us, and my living aunty is warning us to ignore it, but the cat is howling like the devil dog, and my toes are still poking out.

And then it's morning and we haven't slept.

I've cleaned the lounge room of the holy dirt and holy water from the night before and it's calm. My mum is sleeping … and then it begins again.

So picture my mum in boiling lettuce juice, and it scars her belly. Picture her screaming with popping veins and mad eyes. The white priest-man is back and he's trembling because this is not the Eucharist. His belief is in Roman architecture and he left that behind years ago.

11.   CONFUSED?

HOSTESS: Confused?

It happens, girlfriends, in the playground when none of you are watching.

The girls spun me round in rounds and the ground wouldn't stop, and the laughing girls and the laughter of girls threw me off the edge and falling I fell into the pit of your belly, heartbroken.

That reminds me of something I read on the Web last week, on the Woods Hole Oceanographic Institution site:

An active volcano rising more than 4300 metres from the ocean floor in the Sāmoa Islands has been discovered by a team of U.S. scientists earlier this year ... similar in size to Mt Whitney in California, the largest mountain in the U.S.

The volcano has been called Fa`afafine, a Samoan word that they translate as 'wolf in sheep's clothing'.

It seemed an appropriate name since the size of the volcano was a surprise, and wasn't at all what it appeared to be.

I imagined, in this ambiguity, a world that could've existed in us, Mum ... you and me.

I saw you dancing like a man on fire, and me, like your Gary Cooper (who made a film in Sāmoa once and left behind hundreds of adoring Samoan girls because he could), Gary Cooper, spinning girls and vomiting over my grandmother's insolence.

I am not a fa`afafine, But you, so toothless and full of gum you continue chewing your poker game in the vain hope that tonight's winnings will get you and your family out of social obscurity and into the world of television that you blindly bitch-watch so much of.

HOSTESS VOICEOVER: Well, thank you Brian. Very tropical.

12. LIPSTICK LOVE YOU ALL DAHLING!!

'I'm wearing lipstick again. I suck my tongue in remembrance of you — Gary Cooper.' The first and last time I wore lipstick, it was my mother's. I wore it out one night and was approached by several motherless men, weary and worn out from the weight of their fantastic cocks. I got fag-bashed and my lipstick, smudged. 'How can you offer me love like that, my heart's burnt. How can you offer me love like that, I'm exhausted leave me alone.' You ask too much. I'm too tired. You completely forgive the stairwell that leads to our room. You walk the stairs like a movie star. Upon entering, I find a ready poured glass of cold cow's milk (my favourite of all secretions). I am overwhelmed by your powers of suggestion. You turn me on and I don't like it.

Please leave me, children are watching.

Matautia Phineas Hartson
Photograph: Courtesy of contributor

Matautia Phineas Hartson

I wasn't raised fa`afafine I was just an intuitive feminine little boy who loved to sing, dance, draw and daydream.

In my little World of home and family; I was safe, secure and loved. It was only when I left the security of my home that I was thrown into the harsh reality of public education. An outside world; cold rules, it was here that I suffered. I did not fit in.

Outside of my Family, even as a small child, 1970s, Auckland, New Zealand was a place of loneliness, isolation and difference. I was saved by my imagination, the love of my family and the knowledge that I would get through it. One day.

I used to dress up in my mother's clothes as a child, exploring her beautiful dresses, silk kimonos, trying on her jewelry; all as an innocent little boy. I didn't know anything about being 'transgender' or 'cross dressing', all I knew was that dressing up was natural. So I envied my sisters, being free and having all of these amazing dresses made for them, yet I had to make do with stylish but boring boy's clothes. Told 'No! You're a boy!'

School life was hell. It was a lonely period of my life with hours of lunchtimes spent alone; too girly to play with the boys and not girly enough to play with the girls. Again my imagination and creativity got me through the hours, imagining what having friends would be like. Luckily, family was my world.

In 1976 my family moved to a smaller town called Invercargill at the bottom of the South Island of New Zealand.

I spent my intermediate and high-school years there. It was torture. Going to an all boys Catholic school was the worst place they could send a shy, quiet, feminine boy who also had the sporting acumen and coordination of a fruitfly. Because of that I was an immediate target and suffered seven years of psychological torture, teased and name-called, causing me to retreat further.

Ironically they teased me by calling me a girl's name which, of itself, didn't faze me; it was the cruelty with which they teased me that got to me. I was just confused and saddened and hurt to think, why did they hate me so much? What had I done to them to deserve this treatment? I had done nothing to them. I can only guess that they saw my gentleness as a weakness. Who knows, but I still feel the pain of those years and the scars still affect me today.

One of the saving graces was that as the years progressed the bullies dropped like flies. I was brighter than most of them and they inevitably dropped out or left high school.

So I connected education with freedom. It was my ticket out of that hell. Fast forward to university, the gateway to a whole new world of experiences. Lifelong friendships were made. Uni was a place where I was introduced to art, music, dance, bands, education and sex experimentation.

I enjoyed the happiest years of my life during this time. I experienced my first heterosexual sexual encounters and continued 'gay' sex which was still taboo then in the late eighties. Homosexual Law Reform[1] had just been passed but incidents of homosexual bashing and gay venues being firebombed were common occurrences. I still remember the fear of being stuck in a hidden gay venue after someone had thrown a Molotov cocktail through the front door. Again, I just couldn't understand the level of hatred people felt towards us then and even now.

But during that time I felt comfortable enough to come out as gay to my sisters and a small number of close friends. My sisters accepted me and so did my friends but to the outside I remained closeted. It was just not safe enough.

For years I was always attracted to Island men. All I wanted was a nice Samoan husband just like my father and my uncles. I just wanted what my parents had.

But on the gay scene I was disappointed at the 'fast food'

---

1   The New Zealand Homosexual Law Reform Act of 1986.

nature of short-term relationships on offer or the quick sex roundabout. It just wasn't me. I never felt a part of it.

Luckily I did eventually meet the love of my life – a good-looking Niuean named Steve.

It had its rocky beginnings with him being engaged to a woman at the time and being pursued by four different women, but it resulted in twenty-three happy years. I loved him with all my heart. He was Islander, handsome and family orientated. Steve was in the closet; he never came out to his family during our whole relationship. I thought that was an issue; now I don't really think it was. Only in regards to being recognised as his partner.

We moved to Australia together in 1992. In 1994 I came out to my father who, though disappointed, never stopped loving me. Sadly I didn't get the chance to tell my mother as she died suddenly at fifty-four. Gone too soon. But I remember telling her that she was the only woman in my life. I know she knew then.

So, that to many may be the happy ending to my story. No. It's just the beginning.

This year in 2016 my relationship ended.

The last decade I had begun to connect more with being more fa`afafine than 'gay'. I related more and more to being 'fa`afafine' to 'being like a woman' but still acknowledging my maleness. I related to that.

In 1996 I traveled to Sāmoa and stayed for three months. It changed my life.

While in Sāmoa I finally realised that I was fa`afafine in the real and literal sense. I loved it. But I also saw what local fa`afafine didn't see as an outsider.

I saw that being fa`afafine in Sāmoa was not all a bed of roses. I felt that there was still stigma attached to being fa`afafine. You were accepted only in certain contexts and on certain levels but doors were not all open to you.

The more female you were the more sexism you experienced, and as a male presenting fa`afafine you weren't taken seriously, as a straight male was taken seriously.

I felt that positions and roles of responsibility or seniority were given to straight 'married' men first; as fa`afafine we were as 'less than'.

Living in Sāmoa, I also saw how reinforced the pattern to grow up, get married and have children was, to continue that pattern. This is the basis of Samoan society. I saw that fa`afafine are a part of this society but because we cannot conceive or continue that bloodline our role in society is limited.

In regard to relationships, I felt that as fa`afafine in Sāmoa, relationships were often tumultuous and shortlived. There seemed to be an unwritten understanding and expectation that your boyfriend of three years or so would ultimately leave you to get married and have a family. Fa`afafine were seen as the 'entrée' or even the 'dessert' but not 'the main course', so when one short-term relationship ended a new one soon began. But I didn't want that. I wanted the whole thing, the husband, the marriage and the family.

As I mentioned earlier I just wanted what my parents had. Not a big ask, I thought. So when I returned to Australia I lived my life as male as I was happily in a loving long-term relationship with Steve, so I believed I didn't need to change. But after twenty-three years I realised that something was missing. I wanted him to commit to marriage. My partner couldn't do it. So we split after twenty-three years and the following week I started hormone replacement therapy. Steve is still the love of my life and he is blood, my rock, but we are no longer together as a couple.

It has now been a year since I started hormone replacement therapy and I'm happy with the results. I feel aligned to my 'authentic self'. I'm also in a new relationship with a heterosexual man. I don't know how long it will last but I'm happy.

On my transitions I recently decided to tell my father about my becoming female, as I had organised to have partial facial feminisation surgery in Thailand, April 2016.

I wrote him a letter and sat on it for months. I then decided one day to send it. The letter contained how I had struggled with this decision and how I was unhappy as a man and had contemplated suicide the year before even after achieving all that I had achieved. I said that my spirit, my soul, my being was sad and not fulfilled. So I sent the letter.

A few weeks passed and then I received a Facebook message from my youngest sister in Sāmoa to call Dad. The penny dropped. I replied, telling her that I would call him the next day.

So the following day, which I had taken off work, I called my father. Now, my father is an eighty-five year old pastor in a conservative Samoan Evangelist Christian Church.

I said 'Hi Dad!' as I had said countless times before. My father replied immediately; his words shaking and weighed down with emotion. He said, 'Son, I want you to hear these words directly from my lips, I Love you son, no matter what!'

My soul soared leaping into the sky. My heart was instantly filled with so much love for my father at that moment that I felt my chest would burst. We spoke and cried and I talked briefly about my decision.

My father said as long as I was happy, to live my life and not to listen to anyone. I was over the moon. I felt like singing.

Music, in my life, and education they have always been inter-twined. Music during those tortuous years at school saved me. Education saved me also as a way out. My music has always been about love lost, heartbreak, unrequited love, that Billie Hollday kind of love. Being taken for granted and used while in love. I guess I experienced all of those things in previous relationships. Maybe I gave away too much of myself.

One of my songs is called 'Love Supply', about how a loved one used my love supply and how I regained the strength and the love back. It's a happy ending to a relationship that ended badly. But in reality I never really regained that love lost. From life of a gay man in a long-term relationship I experienced sex outside of it. I didn't plan on it but due to a broken heart after my partner cheated on me after seven years I took on the attitude of 'if you can't beat 'em, join 'em.' At that time I didn't leave him, as I still loved him. But it changed the dynamic of our relationship forever.

The gay sex scene was not all easy sailing either: it had many requirements. You had to look a certain way, be gym fit, be 'straight acting', not feminine in ANY way. Be like a man, walk like a man, have a large penis, be the active partner during sex a 'top' or 'versatile'. i.e. be able to do both. AND be rugged, sexy and ultimately WHITE.

So, as a pretty, fat, femme, brown gay guy, I didn't stand a chance. My Pacific exotic gay male card was not valid in Australia. That card, in Sydney Australia, was for Asian men; and the limited Pacific men who were in Australia all predominantly wanted white guys. The same was the case in New Zealand.

BUT as a pretty transgender woman, the social media doors flung wide open. Being a feminine Pacific trans woman was now 'exotic'. Being 'curvy' was a bonus, especially to the men I found attractive; Mediterranean Middle Eastern, Eastern European, Hispanic men. Being beautiful, as opposed to 'handsome', was a blessing.

Pacific men were still elusive to me as a trans woman. They were still afraid to be seen or 'exposed' as being anything other than 'straight'. Generally speaking, Pacific guys had too much personal baggage or religious guilt/hang-ups/mummy issues. So at forty-nine I have no time for that.

But there was a big downside to my newly found popularity as a Pacific trans woman. Those doors, though open, were open predominantly for casual sexual liaisons, not meaningful long-term relationships. It was frustrating chatting to guys who were initially lovely and polite and engaging, but as soon as I disclosed my transgender status the majority turned into sexual predators. They immediately wanted to know if I had a penis and if so, how big? If I had breasts and if so, how big? They demanded I send naked photos of my body immediately, keeping in mind that I had only just met them a few seconds ago. Was I a top, a bottom? The only thing missing were requests to check my teeth. All decorum evaporated and what was left was an ugly engorged penis on the other side of the conversation demanding immediate sexual attention and satisfaction.

At this point I reminded them that I was not interested in casual sex, that what I wanted was if anything a platonic friendship, ultimately leading to a long-term relationship. When I had met my previous partner of twenty-three years I insisted that we wait before we had sex. That had made all the difference, well for seven years anyway, before he cheated on me.

So after telling guys that I wasn't 'easy', some became abusive (I blocked them). Some reverted to begging for sex (blocked). Some, adding insult to injury, asked me if I could either 'look for' or 'introduce them' to one of my many 'tranny girlfriends' who would step in and service these guys at a second's notice (blocked).

How dare I even think that, as a transgender fa`afafine woman, I deserved respect? But I didn't waiver from my goal, I just lowered my expectations and lengthened the timeframe. My friends told me that I should use my time alone to learn to love my own company, to build a relationship with myself. My response to that was this: I know me. I know myself better than anyone else in the world and what I do know is that 'she' loves herself. Yes she makes mistakes. She will put love before her own interests at times, but she, like anyone, is entitled to make those mistakes and learn from them herself. And she does not do 'single' very well.

So, after a few months I met Masoud, my latest partner, through a dating app. We got to know each other over a number of months. We chatted for a few weeks and we met and on the first meeting we had sex. It just happened that way. I was chatting to a few guys at the time also but Masoud slowly crept into my heart over months as we continued to meet and get to know each other. I knew he was seeing other people but at that stage I was okay with that as neither of us was committed.

Fast forward one year: I am now living with Masoud and his brother. I've met all of his friends, introduced to them as his girlfriend, which is a first for me, as my previous partner never introduced me to his friends or family as his boyfriend or partner even though his family knew we were together.

I think before, with my other lover, because both of us were Pacific Islanders we blended into society so well, passing as cousins, that I didn't see it as a big deal. But now I wanted to be recognised.

So with Masoud he's my first Iranian/Persian lover. He makes me happy is all that I can say and I love him and he says he loves me too. It's not perfect and he has a past and a lot of baggage but that's another chapter. So lightning, like love, does strike twice in the same spot sometimes – call it luck or a curse. Who knows?

Now, as for life lessons that I can bestow to the next generation? My advice if anything is to dream BIG and move forward towards that goal. Dream about doing ANYTHING you are interested in and just move towards it. I Love challenges when I've been told 'No. You cant do it!' I just put my mind and heart into automatic and proved to myself that I could do it and went for it. Time is no issue.

I would also advise to not compare your life, your achievements, gifts and talents, to others'. That will ruin your dreams. Every life is different and you don't know their struggles. There is a lot of wisdom in not coveting your neighbor's shit. If you're going to compete: compete with yourself. And don't listen to anyone who tells you to give up. Don't give up on your dream ever! Take one step at a time. Take any failure as a valuable lesson. Learn from it, have a rest, take time off, but always get back up and move forward, towards your goal. Just get up, brush yourself off and do it. Sometimes life's a bitch. I was teased at school for being different. Betrayed by people I thought I could trust. Had my innocence stolen when I was raped at eighteen at a party and mocked; I learnt from those incidents and moved on.

As regards my education and professional career: I repeated a senior year at high school and failed many law papers at uni and repeated them until I passed. It took me eight years to complete my law degree; nearly two years to complete the practical component. I took time off to work to save and just survive. I paid my own way through university supported also by my then partner Steve, which was a blessing. I owe him that.

But at one point when my relationship was near breaking point, I was alone and I was nearly homeless and literally I had no money. Then, I was saved by a kind fellow student. I got there eventually. I just decided that I would not give up until I achieved what I had originally planned, or at least had given it my all and tried my best. There were many times when I wanted to give up my studies and a time when I thought I might not be able to practice as a lawyer because of a previous run in with the law. But luck, and time, were on my side.

When I graduated with my law degree I was the first fa`afafine to graduate at an Australian university with a law degree and the first fa`afafine to be admitted on the roll of solicitors in the NSW Supreme Court and, this year, the High Court and Federal Court of Australia.

But being a lawyer did not guarantee an easy road either. After years of university study, more years of trials were waiting. I had five years of part-time employment, unemployment and uncertainty. Being open about my sexuality came at a price. Today I am working full-time as a locum solicitor in a Community Law Centre on the Central Coast – accepted as a transgender woman and helping people that really need it.

Who knows what life might bring around the corner but at this very moment, I am in a very happy place. So always, always have faith in God, yourself and the universe. I've also battled with serious deep depression, thoughts of suicide and addiction in my life, but in between those personal battles –

I was bestowed the Ali`i titles of Mata`utia from Fusi in Savai`i from my father's (Tuliloa) side.

I was given the Ali`i title Leaupepe Tai Ma Aiono from Fa`asitou`uta from my mother's (Toleafoa) family village.

All this with full knowledge of my being fa`afafine, that is the strength and the love from within my `āiga. I was the son of my father and my mother's son. That was enough. I love them for it and hold these titles in trust for my nephews or, if God willing, my own sons one day. Life as described in the *Forrest Gump* movie is 'like a box of chocolates … you never know what you're gonna get?'

As regards human rights law I advocated for changes to anti-homosexual legislation in Sāmoa, resulting in the laws actually being changed because of my and other advocates' hard work. The lives of fa`afafine were made better because of it.

I was the first president of Oceania Rainbow Network Sydney Australia – a support network for Pacific LGTBIQ in Sydney, Australia. I am also a director of human rights organisation 'Kaleidoscope Australia', advocating for legislative changes to discriminatory LGTBIQ laws in Asia and the Pacific.

I wrote for magazines. Wrote original songs and had them released and played on commercial radio. I even had my five seconds of fame on Australian reality TV show *The Voice* and met Ricki Martin and Kylie Minogue, and now my story is being shared in this book. But now I'm starting a new chapter in my life as a forty-nine-year-old fa`afafine transgender woman and contemplating starting a new business outside of law. I'm excited, thankful and loved by a close-knit family and friends.

Always love life. I have experienced true love in my life twice and have also suffered great loss, but for everything I am thankful and am truly blessed. Alofa atu.

Memea Eleitino Ma`aelopa

I was born on the 10th of May 1946 and grew up in the village of Pesega, which is where the Mormon Church is.

My parents noticed that I was a fa`afafine because when I was growing up I used to do all the girlie stuff most of the time, like helping my mum do the washing, wash the dishes and do the cooking. Only a few times did I help do the umu, which is the part my dad used to do with my brothers. As I grew up I noticed the way I was acting and realised I was more into girl's games like netball. So that's how I sort of grew up and I never regret being a Samoan fa`afafine.

At school, there were times the students in the class noticed my nature and they always said funny things and made funny faces to me about being and acting like girls. But as time went by I said to myself, 'Be yourself. Grow up and do whatever you want, and don't worry about what people say about you.'

The church noticed that I was fa`afafine but I still went to do what needed to be done, and when I came over to New Zealand it was the same thing. It was funny because one of my sisters tried to make sure I didn't act like a girl, and more or less encouraged me to do the boys stuff.

Despite that, some of the faife`au or church pastors probably saw who I was and they ignored it, letting things be, allowing a person to be themselves.

I came to New Zealand in the 1970s; I flew from Sāmoa to American Sāmoa with Polynesian Airlines and came to New Zealand with Pan American Airways. I was staying in Auckland with one of my uncles, quite a few of us staying together. Our extended families came from Sāmoa and as before, we lived together.

In Auckland I used to be a basketball referee at the YMCA, which is sort of how I came to Christchurch in 1984. This

Memea Eleitino Ma`aelopa
Photograph: Courtesy of Lana Shields

happened because I went to the South Pacific Games in Sāmoa in 1983 as a basketball referee, after which I was due to have a knee operation to remove my knee cap because it was ruined from basketball. So I had my operation towards the end of 1983 and I came down to Christchurch to do my physiotherapy, and to just relax and I ended up living down here.

My attraction to Christchurch is that it's nice and quiet and at that time you'd hardly see any Samoans, though there were Samoans around but you wouldn't see them often.

My first job was working at the University of Canterbury helping students search for jobs as an employment officer, and from there I did some studies and did a few papers and moved on to other areas to work.

In Christchurch, I was part of many trusts, boards and funding committees for the government. So, for many years I was involved with the National Co-op committee and the LDC – the Local [funding] Distribution Committee – who work closely with the Department of Internal Affairs.

From there I joined the board for one of the biggest Pacific Island health providers in the South Island, Pacific Trust Canterbury, where I was a board member and treasurer for over ten years. I've also been the treasurer and a patron for the Samoan Student Association at University of Canterbury since 1989.

There's heaps of community groups I've been involved with and helped to set up: Matai o Sāmoa Kalaisitete – it's different from Fono Faufautua or the advisory group, and it's different from Fono a Matai Sāmoa.

The reason why my being Samoan and fa`afafine was never an issue in my work is because I was able to do things other fa`afafines can't do.

In 1998 I was appointed as Justice of the Peace and I do a lot of work in that capacity, helping many of our people with passports and citizenship, and people who come to New Zealand and overstay. I also go to the prisons to help

Immigration [New Zealand] with interpreting. So for me
being a fa`afafine, I can do all these kinds of things. I think it's
an opportunity for us as Samoan fa`afafine to use the skills
that we do have to help our people. My highlight has been
that in 2010 I was awarded the Queen's Medal as Member of
the New Zealand Order of Merit.

I think it's really good for us older fa`afafine to encourage
the young ones to do something for themselves at the Love
Life Fono.[1] Lucky for them that they have the opportunity now,
not like us in those days – we didn't have much opportunity
to come here to New Zealand to do things for ourselves – so
that's why I always encourage them.

I was also one of the first Pacific Island AIDS trainers for the
New Zealand AIDS Foundation where they trained us to go
back to our people to educate them about AIDS. We also had
the opportunity to go to Hawai`i to further our training at the
conferences there.

One of the most difficult situations I have encountered
in my community service work is trying to make our people
understand their rights when they come to New Zealand
planning to overstay. What we do is to make sure they
understand and to make sure they are doing the right thing,
always encouraging them, 'If you can't live here then don't
hang around, make sure you leave before you become an
overstayer so that you can always come back. Because the
more you hang around here you might do stupid things, get
into trouble with the police and the law and then you might
get locked up and that's the easiest way to get deported back.'

That's the kind of thing that's really hard for us because
we feel for our people ... But we have to explain to them their
rights – and even though they know they're wrong, they always
think they're right.

I've helped out many families of overstayers with documents

---

1 Annual gathering of LGBT Pacific people in Aotearoa, sponsored by
   New Zealand AIDS Foundation. Memea is in photograph center.

get their permanent residency and their citizenship through the right channels, and I'm so glad that I was able to help them – all without any payment because, as a JP, I never accept any money or donations for my work unless it's for interpreting. There are heaps of overstayers in those situations, from eighteen-year-olds to the older generations – but what can we do? I cater for Pacific and all people who need my help.

Right at the time that the 2010 Christchurch earthquake hit I was getting my supper, so it was good that I avoided the worst of it, and have since not taken any more office jobs. I'm fortunate that being single and not having any children at the time it happened, I could do whatever I wanted.

My place is still standing but I've had great support from everywhere. We also have a Pacific Hub which is established to help the victims of the earthquake in the east side in Aranui, and that's where I helped out. I didn't go there because I needed money or whatever, but I was there to help our people.

Although I don't have children I have been blessed having nieces and nephews – they are my children and they know that and they always look after me and make sure I'm okay. When the earthquake happened, my nephew was one of the policeman who came to Christchurch to help. He wanted me to come stay with his family in Auckland and I said, 'You know what? You've seen that my place is okay and I'm okay, I'm happy.' But I'll probably visit them later on.

My nieces and nephews accept me for who I am, for being a faʻafafine uncle. Some of them they call me Aunty, which is how our Samoan people always look after us and treat us.

My advice for you faʻafafine is to be yourself and to make sure to: aim high, look ahead and do something better for yourself for your family and for your country.

Shevon Solipo Kaio Matai
Photograph: Courtesy of Fernandez Matai

Shevon Solipo Kaio Matai

My birth name is Solipo Kaio Matai and that's my family name from my mum's side. My mum's Vaosa and she's from Vaimoso[1] and Fagatogo.[2] And my dad is Muaimalae Kaio Matai, he's from Satitoa Aleipata and Satupaitea, Savai`i.[3] I was born here in American Sāmoa and grew up in Fagatogo.

My dad is a very difficult man and he can't speak English. One of my motivation to study English as a second language is because Dad couldn't speak English and I look at him and I know that he's a scholar in Samoan culture and language. And so I wanted to translate for my dad and, taking him to the hospital, that inspired me to study English as a second language, is because of that particular reason. With all the palagi doctors, [he] wanted to understand every single thing that the doctor was saying. So I had to try my best with very limited English skill because Samoan is my first language. For some reason I think that way and I try to explain to Dad what the doctor was saying and I've been doing this since I was ten years old for my dad.

Very very difficult man – it's probably his upbringing from Satitoa Aleipata and you know, back in those back villages of Sāmoa where Christianity is just at its height, men were not allowed to ... actually fa`afafine were banned from the village because they have to cut their hair short. All men had to have their hair short and women wear long hair. So every fa`afafine that wanted to be a fa`afafine and grow their hair and be a woman would have to leave the village and go someplace else and stay. So it's most likely that the village was fa`afafine-free.

---

1 Village in Apia, Sāmoa.
2 Village on the southwestern shore of Pago Pago Bay, now in the center of the city of Pago Pago, American Sāmoa.
3 Villages on the island of Savai`i in Independent Sāmoa.

I'll take that back: I think they were 'feminine fa`afafine'-free –
those who wanted to grow their hair and dress up in girl clothes
was unacceptable, but there were fa`afafine who just cut their
hair and were comfortable with looking like a man.

My dad was very very strict with me and he did not like me
being a fa`afafine at all, at all. In `Upolu, I'm referring to my
dad's village, because my cousin, who is passed – her name is
Keisha Alatise – grew up from Satitoa and Tise had to leave
the village mainly to live her life as a fa`afafine, wearing girl's
clothes. She wanted to live that life so where else to go but to
move to Apia, move to town, place of change where change was
acceptable.

If you were actually going to the villages and understand
it from maybe in the 1970s then you would notice that life for
the fa`afafine has changed a lot [in] establishing SFA [Sāmoa
Fa`afafine Association] in Apia, and SOFIAS⁴ in Pago Pago.
SOFIAS was once Island Queens – a haven. Then there the
change for fa`afafine life through those establishments.

I think fa`afafine in the past had their own standards and
those standards were accepted. I guess I would like to look at
fa`afafine life as how the missionary looked at Samoan culture
that was sexual and how they looked at fa`afafine. Because when
missionaries saw pōula⁵ and it was a very sexual kind of process,
and then Sāmoa disguised it with by saying its pōsiva – just a
night of entertainment. And so it was accepted there: when you
say it was pōsiva,⁶ no more sexual practises with pōula – so they
lose traditional way of pōula but still kept the evening and still
kept that element.

But there were changes, so, with fa`afafine, I think they were
seen as ... you know ... because of the Bible, and the Christianity
and its teaching. So they banned homosexuality: they probably

---

4 Sosaiete o Fa`afafine i Amerika Sāmoa: Society of Fa`afafine in
   American Sāmoa.
5 Bright night, a pagan orgy of dancing, song, and more.
6 Dance night, a Christian evening of dancing, song, and more.

saw that it was there and it was accepted. But then again we have to look at who were the missionaries that came, and there was the London Missionary Society from London and they would understand the fa`afafine from their homosexuality in London and when they were traveling and saw fa`afafines [they] said, oh this is forbidden, you don't do this.

All my life, all my life that my dad put me into all-boys school, mainly because of that reason; but it was a blessing in disguise for me as he put me in there. I hear he talks with people of my family, 'E ave ile a`oga a kama leaga e fa`afafine. And I put in my blessing into it.' So now that I'm old and I think, what were Dad's intentions putting me in school; but of course I knew that Dad wanted me to be in the best school, and I see it that way as well.

When my dad passed away this year everything started to unfold for me. I think my dad knew a life of a fa`afafine and he prepared me for it. He knew what would arm me best to live my life was to get an education. I guess he foresaw things that I would be going through and if I didn't have an education I wouldn't be able to survive.

My dad is dependable and my whole family, the Fa`agata family in Fagatogo, depended on him to take a si`i.[7] Also depended [on him] to do the oratory things. Just the depth of [how] he sees the Samoan language and how he taught his kids to see Samoan language through his eyes. I don't know who would ever see culture the way Dad does and [the] very deep sense where he would be poor and he would also rather be hungry, in the culture. That kind of perception and that kind of mentality was important for him. And then some of his writing I read and I hear it from all around; they said, your dad speaks aloud well with Samoan language. Young Women's Christian Association invited him to speak as a scholar. So there are a lot of instances where it proved to me that Dad was a scholar in Samoan culture and language.

My mum was my protector. She knew my life and she knew

---

7 A ceremonial gifting, often connected with a malaga or traveling party.

I was a fa`afafine because she is from two towns: her dad is from Vaimoso, a town in Apia, and her mum in Fagatogo town in Tutuila. So Mum knew about me. She passed when I was fourteen. But growing up with Mum – I don't know how to explain, but I was a very happy child around my mum and she is a designer and seamstress and I loved doing things with her growing up. Sew and put rhinestones on wedding dresses – because she sewed wedding dresses. And go to the store and buy the glues; and there were these three to four prongs for the diamonds where you press it from the bottom and you put the diamond on the top and close the prongs.

She was very creative and I kinda followed her with that. I did a lot of the designing with her back in Sāmoa, in Miss South Pacific. I knew how to do all of these things from her, like taking a box, cut it and all of a sudden there is a hat that came out of the box and she would sew the material around it and so when it's done it's a hat. Trim shoes with flowers to match with the outfit.

My days with Mum I would fall asleep while she is sewing something at night and I would wake up in the morning and there is a beautiful dress right in front of my eyes. She is sleeping from working all night and this is what I see every single day. Sew clothes for everybody, and she was a very popular local seamstress designer. She designed for Nora Coleman, the governor's wife. She won a lot of funfairs and every prize she gets was a Singer sewing machine and she gave it to her sisters because my mum's family had an upholstery business in Vaimoso. So she grew up like that … And there were only two boys – my brother and I.

When my dad beats me up she will take the beating too to protect me. Literally she will lie on the top of me and take the beating. I would be walking to present his food and I would get a slap or something and realised it was the way I walked. And my hair never passed my neck ever; he made sure he cut it. The way I wear my clothes, the clothes I wore, these are the things he made sure I don't step out of line. I would tuck my shirt with my `ie faitaga and my tie or my bow tie to church, tuck in my shirt to my shorts or ʻie faitaga for school, never get to go away – it's like I have to wear what he was wearing.

Age four or five, I knew I was faʻafafine, because of the ECE[8] – it's almost like a 'headstart' in Samoan Aoga Faʻataʻitaʻi before you go to the regular elementary – during Aoga Faʻataʻitaʻi, I was interested in playing with the dolls, doing the suʻiga ʻula[9] and dancing, and these are the things I can remember. It was okay with the teacher; I was more … I enjoyed their laughs and I enjoying their laughs … happy happy times when I get up to do the siva … I would hear the laughter and the laughter grew with me, you know, and still is.

And if anybody now, with the faʻafafine generation, they would yell back, as they take that laugh as an insult now. But when I grew up with the laugh it was a beautiful laugh, it was a happy laugh – until I come to realise that they are laughing not so much at the talent but they are laughing at my personality, my character as a faʻafafine. That's where I kinda like thought that it was offensive at first … But I'm one of the people that ignore the laugh, you know – I ignore it but I have friends that pick up on it.

But that's when I was at Aoga Faʻataʻitaʻi and got up and siva. We sewed our leis and have a nap and wear the lei and do a siva and everyone does the siva before you go home and I'm always making people around me laugh.

Faleaitu,[10] you would have to perform to get the laugh, but with faʻafafine you come with the laugh … So I'm so fortunate to be a faʻafafine because it brings laughter to the life of the people and I would like to see it that way rather than an insult. I don't see that laugh that way like an insult to me.

Now I'm old and when I look back at my life, it drives me to be good at my talent. When I'm dancing and the laughter grows,

---

8 The American Sāmoa Department of Education (DOE) Early Childhood Education (ECE) Program.

9 Sewing party for making of ʻula or leis from leaves and flowers.

10 Samoan comedy story telling with characters, sometimes fa'afafine characters.

I do more stuff just to hold that happiness – all that laugh it's coming from me; all that energy it's from me.

Funny that my dad see it the way I see it because every time I go out in public – I don't know why but I guess I do with, you know, those gangster boys in the mainland, you know – they see you, they would say things and kinda laugh. But when I go with my dad there was this one time that when I was with my father that I'm totally a different person when I'm around my dad because the laugh would make my dad upset because that laughter to him is an insult and very degrading.

Yes to him but not to me. I would like the laugh when I'm by myself but when I'm with him like, inside me, when I'm with my dad I'm like, 'Please oh please don't laugh at me.' And there is this laugh that would always come out. But if people know that, knew my dad was a very strict man, they won't.

I have eight sisters and two brothers. My family they are all college graduates. I don't know but I feel like I was always ahead of myself – I kind of like knew things like before I was supposed to; that kind of feeling, like I knew how to make love and have sex before I was supposed to have sex.

My first encounter was with a cousin of mine, he was a cousin of mine … That first encounter stays with me, the smell of the place we went. Still now it will turn me on any time of the day I would smell the wood and flower, it's an aphrodisiac, I'm aroused when I smell wood – and you know, when I go to buildings and they are building these fales and I smell the wood, I'm instantly turned on and because of that very first encounter – that's when I sucked my first cock. I didn't know I was supposed to put it in my mouth and then I encounter and it was pleasurable and that, do what I'm doing, no emotions involved it was just performing.

When we were playing football rugby with my cousins that were of my age, with the one I had it with for the very first time, was older than me. Boys my age, we were playing football rugby tackling and contacting with each other [and he] fell on the top of me and I felt different but [what] was funny for me is that I felt different and he felt different falling on me ... So that was my first feeling of sexual encounter.

My mum dressed me up while Dad goes to work. My sister works at the bank, had all those hairpieces [that] in the seventies were part of the femininity and beauty. And mum sew, and the mirror, the makeup was all over and I would be playing with the makeup and my sister's hair pieces, looking at them. And I had eight women in the house, oh my gosh. And so Mum would laugh at me coming down with big heels while she is sewing and next thing I knew she had sewn my top and I would do my fe`aus with my top. Here in American Sāmoa there is a siren in town from the Van Camp Cannery, at 4pm it goes woooo, and my mum would say, 'Eh! Go take off! Dad is going to come home', when she hears the siren.

I never called my father Dad, back then I called him by his first name. But I called my mum Mama. I called my dad Kaio because there was a wall in front of all the children and him. We had to go through our mum to tell him what we needed. No one went ahead and asked him. My father was a carpenter and never had fa`afafine friends. My parents never had fa`afafine friends, just one fa`afafine but not dressed as a woman. My role models were my sisters and my mum.

When I had my first sexual encounter with Loia my cousin. He tells everybody that I was his first break – because Tasha told me that [Loia] said I was his first break and he told me that it stayed with him too. It's funny, he fell on me and I fell off, because he came and said to me to come to the house. And he pulled me over and kissed me and he told me to 'suck my dick', and I did and I liked it. From then on the sky was the limit with all the church boys and that's when I discovered myself.

Going to school and seeing other fa`afafine friends maybe hiding to themselves ... But what really worries me is that they're talking like, 'eh!' like it was a no-no. We were talking about these guys, but they don't do anything with them. I was the one ahead of my time and having sex with them and going to all-boys school with fa`afafine we were mostly treated like women of the school at Marist Brothers Elementary in Atu`u and Marist Brothers High School in Malaeloa.

I was actually the tāupou[11] for the whole school and I danced at the malae[12] for Flag Day.[13] I was the one that did the taualuga.[14] That's how special fa`afafine were at Marist. I had no title, no position for any class of school, I wasn't even a student body rep but, because I was a fa`afafine and I knew how to siva I got that taualuga. So it's a special title and special performance in Sāmoa and they gave it to me. I danced for Marist in 1985 and all the other girls were Miss Samoana, Miss Leone and Miss ASCC.[15] They had titles, they were beautiful girls, so I saw it that way: I was the Miss for Marist Brothers when, you know, there are no Miss for an all-boys school. I wore boys' school uniform and used colored chalks as eyeshadows; it was beautiful colors, it was colorful.

I was the youngest to win the Miss Island Queen title. Fagatogo in my village in Pago Pago; they had a Hollywood and Beverly Hills. They are houses full of fa`afafines. I was so fascinated by people who were like me. So although my house was the cleanest house, I would look for the trash just to walk past their house to look at them. Because I would be walking in the middle of the road between Hollywood and Beverly Hills and I would hear drums! Laughing! Hearing tones of voices screaming! And I would hear a lot of guys in there, it was where guys would love to go, it was beautiful.

Hollywood actually came from `Upolu, you know; Apia's safe haven was Hollywood, where they migrated, because Apia was one of the places that had a law where men weren't allowed to wear women's clothes. So they migrated here. So they brought Hollywood here. Natives of this island created Beverly Hills. And

---

11 Ceremonial girl chief.
12 Village green for ceremonies.
13 Colonial holiday in American Sāmoa.
14 Taupou dance at high point in ceremonies.
15 Samoana High School, Leone High School; ASCC is American Sāmoa Community College.

these places were literally known for where actors and actresses lived and that's their life and that's how it was created, because these fa`afafine wanted to be glamorous actors and actresses and they really lived up to the glamor.

Men of status would go and meet them there and the governors would talk about it. All the fa`afafines in the back villages would try and move there because they heard of the place. Today those houses are still there but no longer called Hollywood and Beverly Hills. But at Hollywood, which was a Samoan fale, there was one fa`afafine living there because it was her family house, and the family let other fa`afafine live there because their sewing production was bringing in money, so they kept them there.

Those days it used to be filled with Samoan men because it was Fagatogo where all the bars were. So then, when the men were drunk they would go there to have sex. The fa`afafines had standards of selecting their men. It would be over money kinda thing, that's why men of status would go there – it was not prostitution, it was never seen as prostitution but as a life of a married couple where men would bring money and food to the house. They would immediately play a role of a woman and a husband for a very short time before he goes back to his real wife and kids and there ends the episode of the day, and the next day comes with a new episode and a new man. It's playing actress; would act normally, it's very natural, natural:

'Hun, au mai le mea`ai.'

'Did you come with food? What did you bring?'

'I brought some chicken.'

``Ia, leave it over there I'm gonna come and cook it.

'What did you wanna eat?'

So fa`afafine would cook food, have sex and he leaves.

Those at Hollywood and Beverly Hills had jobs – like Dr. Vena Sele and Leroy Lotu, those were the ones had teaching jobs. They were professional women and had relationship with men of status. I always wanted to live there in that arrangement, that arrangement it fit me, that's why I would take out the trash just to see it. And when they, Hollywood and Beverly Hills, would see me, and say, 'Leai `ua sau! Lea `ua sau!' and call out the drum roll and I would drop the trash and do the tamure! And they invited me into the house and it was really magical life and magical world.

That was the core conversation, was, 'Fai tatou mea lea. We are all women and we have our husbands,' like a role-play, and you would come in and take part in the role-play and everyone would get up and move around the house, 'What are you doing?' 'I'm cooking.' This role-plays just came out of nowhere. But in normal life of the houses there is a Mama and an Aunty Mama, all these terms. The Mama would be the older fa`afafine and Aunty Mama would be the aunties but little bit more than an aunty. Aunty Mama because you would go to them for things like how you would go to your mama ... And I was called a 'small mala.'

'Mala' is another term for fa`afafine. It was actually coined by the heterosexual community and it means 'cursed' – 'You're a cursed mala.' And when the fa`afafines were called a mala the fa`afafines liked it, they never saw it as a curse but as another name for fa`afafine. It hit me that, when I heard it from fa`afafine in Apia, how many times did we not use that word mala: it was [a] statement that made me think that the word was sour to me and the word fa`afafine was also sour to me. My dad my family my church people were like, 'Eh! Fa`afafine!' It was very degrading ... but 'mala' was more of a joking word. 'Fa`afafine' literally meaning 'the way of the woman' and 'mala' literally meaning 'cursed', so we were more slanted towards adopting 'mala' than 'fa`afafine.' Now, with the association [SFA] being established, the fa`afafine word has come easy to the mind.

Coming to college was almost like a something that just happened. I left Marist Brothers High School at my senior year because my grades were dropping really bad. I was going to school just to see the boys, and lived that imaginative life of having a boyfriend: that was important to me than anything else.

My dad find out that I wasn't making my grades so he took me out of Marist. He said, 'You're not going to school ever. I think it's best for you to stay home, do the umu and do the guy chores,' and it was that night I was massaging my dad till three o'clock in the morning and then, like all parents, they felt bad for me. So the next day he said, 'Okay, I guess you have to go to Samoana High School.'

So that's when I went to Samoana High School and Leroy was there, the famous fa`afafine in Fagatogo. Leroy was the one that put me through school and watched over me. That was Beverly Hills, because he owned Beverly Hills. Leroy doesn't dress up. They accepted him more. He never married but adopted a son. He was another relationship girl and he has a relationship as we speak. Leroy was more of a father figure fa`afafine, and Vena was a mother figure fa`afafine.

Aside from my life at home and how home shaped me, my life, with Vena and Leroy and the fa`afafine, took a whole different shape. I was shaped by that life to understand both worlds. They pretty much shaped my education. I saw Vena and Leroy and how they lived their life and how money was never a problem to them because they were single and they lived their life. So I wanted that kind of life and I wanted to be like them, independent, have a job, do what you can. There was a freedom and I kinda saw the freedom I didn't have back then because my dad was constantly on my case.

I came here at ASCC in 1987; I graduated in 1986 from Samoana and I went to college in 1987. My first job was working as work-study here on campus. There was a program called JTP [Junior Training Program], and I started work as tenth grader and twelfth grader at Junior JTP. It was for students to go into the work field and I worked at a bingo because it was more a fa`afafine job.

I went to Hawai`i to get away from my dad to get away from the beating. I was only twenty-two. I got the hose, the back of the machete; just imagine going to elementary with bruises on your face. All my siblings were getting it but I was always the one that was into exploring and being the independent one. I was the one that played sports. I played rugby and football. In track, I'm a runner – our team at Marist won seven years straight. I ran 800 miles, so I played a lot of sports. It was getting me away from the house and going places with my friends and it was really outgoing that got me into all these games. One game my dad got me into was baseball, the Little League: he bought my uniform and he liked me playing sport – but he didn't like it when I played games and didn't come home to do my fea`us. I play any game.

At twenty-two I went to Hawai`i and told my dad I was going to school. That's when he accepted me because I was going to school. I stayed with my cousin – oh no, I cannot stay with fa`afafines; I stayed with my cousin. When I got there my dad called because at the time now, to him, he seen people around him – all families are doing was going off the island to go to school overseas was the highest role and that was the goal. But when I left the island I didn't go for school but because I wanted to live a freer fa`afafine life. I wanted to be a woman, that's what I wanted to be.

So after one week since my arrival my dad called and said to my cousin, 'Va`ai, fa`alelei le kama,' meaning take care of the boy, and he said, 'Let me speak to him.' So my cousin gave me the phone, and he said, 'Listen here, you're not coming back until you get that degree. Don't ever think about coming back home, you stay there until you get it, then you see me. That is your ticket to coming back to the family.'

And that's why I went to look for a college. I really didn't take it much that time because that's what I wanted in the first place, which was never to return, which I wanted. And that's what I wanted to hear, so I can call and say, 'I'm not done.'

After seven years I graduated in 1993 with Bachelors in English as a Second Language. Funny, going to the university after hanging out with Dad. And I said to myself, I got to do something with this, I got to just say that I'm still at school. But I guess Dad nailed that in all of us that I didn't want to lie to my dad, so I registered with a university although I was barely passing. I just wanted to get through and it wasn't my intention to excel. I didn't want an A; and if the passing grade was C, I do C, that's all I wanted. That's how I went to school and I regret it because now with the profession that I have I wished that … because I could honestly say that I went to school sleeping, because I never put my one hundred percent foot forward.

My one hundred percent went to entertainment, to my fa`afafine life, dancing here, choreographing things. When I was in Hawai`i, I was one of the very few Samoan fa`afafine that went to the show queen pageant. I was a contestant in Queen of Queens. I went to California International. But it was the schooling and my dad saying, 'Don't come home until you get that degree' that kept me coming back to this.

When I found out that I can dance, I can sing, I can entertain, and pageant was the life and that was the more fa`afafine life and transgender life 'i kuā,'[16] its pageants, and all the girls live for that. They go on the streets to get money for that, to look good in pageants; they spend more money on their costume than the prizes. You're not even there to gain money, you're actually there running just to be on stage. The prizes are not up to ten thousand dollars and they're spending more than that. The girls fundraise throughout the whole year. The money wasn't the issue, because talent was much more important than anything else.

The excitement of being watched is the reason why I do it. People looking at me, their eyes on me, is what kept me going; and to design the best, and to look the best, and to be watched, and to be laughed at in a good way. The cheers you get, I heard when I was a child. I like it. I never entered the pageants for the money or where fa`afafine would dress up. I wanted to go to the pageants to perform and be myself and gain an audience with watchful eyes that are responsive to the things I'm doing and that they like it.

I'm a long-term relationship kinda girl. I've had long-term relationship with palagi men mostly, but a Samoan guy I was

---

16 'I kuā' – back in the village life.

with, I never knew we were going to be living together for nine years and we rented the house with him. I think all my adulthood life went with him. I met him in 1997, April, Flag Day; I finished college already, returned from Hawai`i, and we met here and we stayed here.

Fa`afafine relationship is not seen as a gay relationship – they are more like man–woman relationship. But he loved me for me, he did not care what people would say about us – so, just like a palagi man, and that's why I dated palagi guys – because they understand and be willing to put aside that insulting laugh and love me for me and be with me. And it's hard to find a man like that in Sāmoa, but there are men that would accept you as a fa`afafine and live with you here. I was surprised that the relationship actually went for nine years and I met his family – the mother and the father and the sisters and the brothers. He's the eldest, and when we returned back to our home I said to him, 'Are you alright?' He said, 'Don't worry about it, I told them this is who I want to live the rest of my life with.'

But when my dad got sick and I got the contract to go work in Hawai`i, I took my dad with me and my partner went to New Zealand and got married there. But every time I came to New Zealand he would come and see me and make love to me. He has one daughter. That's when I knew that my relationship with him was totally different than the relationship with his wife, because he sees me not as how I thought he saw me, a 'wife'; he didn't see me as his wife, he saw me as a fa`afafine.

I have a Masters in English as Second Language. I'm fluent in both languages. The Samoan that I learnt from my dad wasn't so much of the general Samoan speaking that I hear. It was his syntax that caught me with the way he said things, it was very simple and the meaning was different; that's what caught my eye with dad's sermons and dad's oratory speeches and the way he would speak to us.

The difference between Samoan language and English language is the structure and pattern is different, in cases of speech. The thinking is different in the way that Samoan language is well intact and attached to the culture. The words are attached to respect and so speaking sort of come that way and writing also sort of come that way. You don't just write but you have to write and be careful of your syntax and the placing of your words that don't offend your reader. When you are in that small box your thinking is not out there, you're not writing; but your writing, because you're trying to keep a respectful writing with your audience and trying to please your audience in a certain way – that's the kind of Samoan writing I get.

Even when I write in English I still carry that Samoan respect with my writing. I have to be very watchful with how I place words because I don't want to offend whoever I'm writing to or the readers. Whereas in English when you write, you just write with a free soul, maybe with strategies that you use, probably the only thing in your mind. But for me, in Samoan, I will always have that respect in my writings.

I wrote a paper on Fa`afafine and Polari, to compare fa`afafine slang with Polari, that English gay language. I called it in my paper fa`afafine slang. I was amazed at how similar the languages are, and both languages happened at all different parts of the world. I was amazed that we also have a back slang. For example, like with the word 'alu' in Samoan for fa`afafine would be 'lu`a'; the 'lu' would be swapped with the 'a' – and the purpose of this fa`afafine slang was mainly to be different and to disguise what you're saying to bystanders, to people that are listening in.

I understand that because fa`afafine have encounters with men of status, and when they talk about it they have to talk about it in a private way. So in order for them not to have the people putting their noses in their business, this slang came in handy to talk about their nights with men of status. So they would talk about it and laugh and talk about what went on and be fa`afafine through their conversation, through using the fa`afafine slangs, because they are the only one that knows it.

This slang, now all students in this generation are speaking it. The whole purpose of the paper was more like awareness to the Samoan public to know that fa`afafine slang is not a language that will replace the informal Samoan language, because it's already keeping in like a vine. Well, [now] the kids are speaking the language and they are speaking like it's theirs. They don't even know the purpose of the fa`afafine language but when they say it, it's like they belong to a certain society, and a society where, when you're there, you're cool. Because when you speak the fa`afafine language you belong to a certain society.

They would use 'Samunda' for 'Samoan'; that will be using similar words to Samoan words. One of the ways they coin words is using the English language because, in Samoan words, you don't end Samoan words with consonants, you always have to end with a vowel; so you would use different suffixes to end words like 'malo', and fa`afafines would turn it into 'malocious' and speak it with that hybrid language, the fa`afafine language that would come and go, and change.

When I went back to Hawai`i in 2005, I got a contract on the trip, which separated my long-term relationship and me. I went to Hawai`i and I brought my dad for his medical; I got this contract at the same time Dad was getting sick so it worked well. I told him, 'Okay, you have to come with me; I have a year contract so you need to stay here for a year. I don't want to be here and you're there and I hear things that you're getting sick and I cannot leave here to come to you.'

But he did not listen, he flies back and forth. So from a father I ran away from, I was taking care of him and it felt very good: my life completed when I took care of my dad. Because I was there when he could no longer walk and all the way up to being bedridden, and I took care of Dad all the way through. He was walking all the way through, in a wheelchair, then bedridden, and Dad died at eighty-two. I have another fa`afafine nephew, my sister's son, who helped take care of Dad while I was able to go to work.

One of my sister's son is a hermaphrodite, she has a vagina and a penis; she lived as a fafine. My dad accepted her more than he did me. I wanted to understand Dad's thinking. I don't know if Dad saw it as a punishment when Fernandez was born that way, because he was all of a sudden very different when he found out that Fernandez was born with two parts – that Fernandez was a true fa`afafine. I liked it that Dad didn't treat her like he treated me, but at the same time I felt different that Dad was more accepting of her than me.

It was hard in the beginning but then I had to understand. What eased my mind about it was that I'm Dad's direct son and there are only two of us, and I understand how it was miserable for Dad to have two sons and not one – and one is fa`afafine and, being fa`afafine, your line stopped with you. If you're really living your life as a true fa`afafine you don't have sexual intercourse with a girl. Your line actually dies with you; it doesn't go anywhere. I see Fernandez doing things that I'm doing, designing, and these are the things she likes. She lives in Hawai`i. She came for Christmas, we took care of Dad, and she flew back and forth; we treated her like Dad's representative.

And I know that because when I'm with Dad, you know, when something bothers him he will look at me and love me – but something bothers him which, I know, it's me being fa`afafine and he's probably doing his own imagination, wishing that I had a wife and kids and living his heterosexual lifestyle. I saw it at times when I'm talking to Dad, I see it – all of a sudden he looks away … but he will never tell me that's the reason why. He knew I was graduating that semester because he died on March 23rd and I graduated in May. He almost made it, yeah, but he knew, and I said to Dad, 'I'm graduating this semester,' so he held on, held on, held on, until he couldn't hold on anymore. But he was happy, he knew I would finish, and when he passed I finished. This was just last year.

So when I went on a journey with my dad for the forty-plus years of my life … Everything now, since my dad died, everything opened up … I understood my life after him, I started to understand the reason why he did things like this to me – [it] was not [that he] disapproved of my fa`afafine lifestyle … My thinking of the things he did went from literal reasoning to understanding it from a bigger picture: Dad did shape and get me ready to live a life as a fa`afafine. And I thank that man for preparing me. I never, never thought that his strictness, and all this treatment that I always saw it as a negative, would prepare me to live the toughness of a life of a fa`afafine in a heterosexual community. I can say that Dad well prepared me to live life. And December of Christmas last year, it was the first time my dad say in Samoan, 'Ai lava o lou olaga lava lea.'[17]

He said it to me and he turned to my sister and said, 'Va`ai fa`alelei lo`u atalii o lona olaga lea mea ia o lona olaga ele toe suia.'[18]

While he was touching my hair I was lying on his bed and he was sitting next to me and he was saying that in Samoan, 'Ai a o lou olaga lea, ole mea lea ete mana`o iai.'[19]

He said that to my brothers and my sisters, and when he died I knew that was my acceptance; for the very first time that was my acceptance from him. It was a blessing. And that man from day one till his passing he never said, 'I approve', which are the words I was looking for, 'Oute talia lou olaga, I approve of your life.' I was more looking for that and never notice that he already approved it with everything that was coming to me, everything that he was doing – that was his approval. It didn't come in one sentence; the approval came throughout my whole life. I missed it and I missed seeing it, maybe because I was growing up and maybe I was too young, my mind was too small to understand.

But now that my dad died and is gone I look back and [I see] this old man knew I was going to be by myself, and here are the things that he lined for me, and that was his approval. I was waiting for him to look at me and tell me that – but that's not what it was. It wasn't that I never understood it … So funny that when I said that, when my dad died last year, it means that the journey of understanding my life has just started … And I think

---

17 'Finally, your life is complete.'
18 'See how well your brother in his life with this has turned his life around.'
19 'In your life with this you have fulfilled all that I wished for you.'

you interview me right at the right time because this is every single time I'm learning and understanding the life as I go along. I'm now more solid with my life because I do things knowingly that these are the things that I wanted. And I'm dressing up freely because these are the things that I wanted: I wanted this life for a long time.

Right now I have discovered that there is too many freedom. I wanted this freedom and it's too much; too much freedom. I teach English here at the Department of Language and Literature at the American Sāmoa Community College. This is my first semester and I love teaching and teaching is always the fa`afafine's life. Well I taught a dance course at the University of Hawai`i for almost two years and I taught with Oceania – they have an Oceania program at the music department and I taught that course at the college level.

That's where my whole full one-hundred-percent went to, not to school, remember, not to school – and I love that part of me, the Arts in me. I'm one of the people that revived the tuiga, the traditional headdress, and I'm the co-founder of the Taupou Manaia dance group – all those dances and the big numbers I taught them.

The first semester here is intense but I like it, I think I belong here. One thing that I never lose, that I taught as a fa`afafine dressing up, is respect. I don't know why – maybe the tone of my voice is low and I speak a little bit more authoritative at times probably. But this laughter – the laugh I was talking about – it's still there, but not at unnecessary times. The first thing I do when I get a fresh bunch of students on the very first day is to establish my ground rules. I move right into, 'I'm the boss. My rules are, follow my syllabus very closely, and what you learn is what you're going to read, so that's basically it. You fall off the wagon, you fall off.'

I think I want to say that fa`afafine are fascinating creatures and their lives are lived on the surface and they belong to be lived on the surface of life. When you go to try and understand fa`afafine in the deeper sense their life is void, because it's [by] going deep that you miss the whole life of the fa`afafine – because you don't need to go very, very, deep to understand a fa`afafine. And many time people try to find out, what is a fa`afafine? How come you're that way? All these difficult questions and all these research are starting to come out about fa`afafine, which is good ... But I believe that you don't have to look too far to understand who we are because it's right there, you just have to have the right eye.

Jean Melesaine

I was so lucky to have my name Jean; it's such an asexual name. When I was younger my teacher would say, Hey are you a boy or a girl? Or they'd say Jean like 'John'; I'd say are you fucking kidding me what kind of brown kid is named Jean like that. My sister her name was Apiseta, and then she was Jennifer because my parents had to assimilate. I was the first kid not to learn Samoan, they were like you are not going to learn that shit, we were have fucking Americanised lives.

My parents' names, my mother her name is Masina Sopo Matai`a Leasiolagi. Leasiolagi, is my father's father's name that I was told could mean orgasm, oso means jumping and lagi means heaven, it could be like jumping heaven. My dad is Moaseni Tito Melesaine. My mom told me that my dad's dad, he was a songwriter, Tito Leasiolagi, *Falealili Uma*, I love that song too, the *Falealili Uma* song. Every time I hear that song, it's such a beautiful song. The acoustic version every time I hear it, it could bring me home.

With my mom, when my parents listen to Samoan music, it's their only way to travel back to their country, living in America. When my mom sees me sing that song, it makes her want to cry, because we'll all play it, even though all her kids are assimilated in American culture, for her to hear us sing a Samoan song it makes her feel okay to be in America, that her kids are going to be okay, they'll always be Samoan forever. I played that song early in the morning when we're eating breakfast. I'm trying to teach my nieces and my nephews. My mom was amazed that everyone knew what that song. It makes me super proud of where I'm from, it's one of those songs, where everything is in slow motion.

I was the only child that didn't go back to Sāmoa, last year was the first time, it was the best thing I could do for myself.

Though I almost died over there. I went to take a picture, my cousin shewas graduating from theology school in Malua, and in Malua they say never go into the water for whatever reason. But I see this guy he's fishing, it's the most beautiful scene and photograph you could ever take. I say okay, it must be okay because he's fucking fishing in the water, so I go into the water, take off my shoes, come back up right by the shore and then I get bit by this fish. They called it a Nofo, a sand fish that killed hella kids because their bone gets infected and they die. Worse shit I could ever do in my life but I guess it was worth it.

You know they don't have no ambulance in Sāmoa so we had to pull someone to the side. I was literally dying; I was pulling my hair, saying Fuck I'm going to lose my leg! I felt like I got cut by a rock, I didn't feel it right away, it's like traveling up my leg, a million pins and needles stabbing my leg. At the hospital they drugged me up. My mom knew something was going to happen. My mom and my aunt, they do Samoan herbal medicine, that shit infected my leg, but it made me feel better, really numbed my pain. I was in bed for a week. I just carried on, limping; I'm the kinda person to do that. I was like; Let's go in the jungle. They were like; Shut up and go to bed. I just carried on.

My parents were immigrants. My father was from Falealili, my mother from Moamoa by the post office in Apia. Falealili, that coastline, it's beautiful, by Fagaloa. I went to a prize giving for my niece, flyest teacher I've ever seen, I really wondered if she was queer, I was trying to give her the queer eye, where you just stare at them and smile, and if they smile back. I'm going to go back.

When my sisters went, they were thirteen they were super immersed into this American culture, being young hood girls in America, they fucking hated Sāmoa, they were like, I want to go home, didn't want to take a shower outside. It was perfect timing for me to go home at this age, to go to Sāmoa see where my parents are from, where I'm from.

My parents didn't meet in Sāmoa they met in America. My dad his mother was going through a lot of mental health issues,

Jean Melesaine
Photographer: Kari Orvik

and I really believe it was my fucking grandfather; she just had a broken heart. My dad dropped out of third grade, because he had to take care of his mom, this is like a country troublemaker. She sent him to Hawai`i when he was a teenager, stayed with his missionary cousins who were Mormon, they lived a college life, and he was a very handsome dark man with really nice features, hella exotified in Hawai`i by white women. He said he didn't speak English but all the women loved him.

My mom she got super exotified when she came to America. She came over with a white man for a job as a housekeeper but ran away because he tried to sexually assault her. My dad came to Oakland to plant the palm trees in front of the Mormon Temple. He went to a cricket game in San Francisco, and he met my mom.

Then they moved to L.A., had my older brother. My older brother passed away when he was a baby in Sāmoa, she took him back, and then they moved to San Jose. My mom's family they're all medicine women, they fofō people, very superstitious. Still trying to present a Christian background but still carry on with indigenous rituals. They think since they named my brother after my grandfather that the child was cursed. Then they had two sisters, then me, then two younger brothers. After me, my parents got married.

San Jose: crazy stuff. We lived on the Eastside, at Kollmar. My mom saw the manager get shot by his girlfriend, a lot of drama. But they really loved the community of immigrants, hella didn't speak English both of them, my sister didn't speak English. This community of different cultures, full of immigrants, full of single parents, it was very hard to find someone that had both parents. Hella kids, a neighborhood that was super amazing, best neighborhood you could grow up in. I had a very good short childhood. The place it looked old and brown and terrible. Because my Mom was an immigrant there was no way out for her with no papers because she came on a work visa from the white dude but it expired.

She would sew these dolls for random people, sew their

clothes to make money, do hella random ass shit, make us do hella random shit with her. She's that mom pushing her kids in a grocery cart, picking up cans along the way, while my dad worked at Jack in the Box, Red Lion, all these random ass places. They were true immigrants. So I have a huge connection with immigrant communities. It's very beautiful thing to see my parents come from that.

When my mom had issues with my dad, because there was domestic violence, what could she do, she was the only one in her family in America. I used to catch my mom on the staircase covering her face crying. I didn't know what was going on at the time. I was very young. And my dad was my hero when I was young, I was super close to him, I was his little boy. My father was my hero when I was young, came to my basketball games, was proud of me, my mother never came, she felt like she couldn't be there because she didn't speak English and didn't want the other parents judging her. He would always take me and my mom would take my oldest sister and younger brother. It was like teams for my parents, their relationship was very unhealthy; we lived like a facade in the Mormon Church.

We were the only Samoans in that complex. And at the church it was all Samoan. It was a forty-minute drive to church, that's how I gained all these aunts and uncles in San Jose, through the church. That community at Kollmar it was a lot of Korean immigrants, her best friends were the Puerto Rican, Mexican and Black families. A lot of her best friends, one of them committed suicide, another one OD'd, most of their kids were my friends, and my mom hella loved those kids. It was one of those neighborhoods you could always ask for sugar, everyone knew everyone who lived in the complex, even if they didn't have kids there were elderly people, everyone was working class, some people worked at the flea market. So when I was young I grew up with these snooty ass Koreans who had more than me and my family. I hella understood class because they'd always taunt us for not having whatever. I'd always play basketball, I hung out with the boys a lot. I was like a boy.

I used to get babysat by one of Mom's friends, then she was in rehab for a hella long time, her daughter was my best friend Mary Jane. I remember this little Korean kid, he must have been five; he said about my friend Mary Jane, 'I don't want her to come in my house because she's dirty.' I said, 'Why's she dirty?' He said, 'Because she's black.' I said, 'That's not right; don't say shit like that.'

I was the leader of the pack. I was eleven. A lot of it stems from being queer and going to church. They gave me this pamphlet it said, 'Homosexuality, You're Not Going to Enter the Kingdom of God.' I knew clearly when I was young that it didn't matter what I did I wasn't going to Heaven. I thought, I guess I'm going to Hell.

Now I'm older I have the language to understand things. But when I was younger I thought, Fuck that's just the way life is, I have two immigrant parents who are poor and I'm not going to enter the kingdom of Heaven, so I might as well do whatever the fuck I can do.

My pack was my younger brother and another kid, we'd hang out with the thirteen-year-olds, okay let's save our two dollars try and get a forty,[1] drink with them. It's funny now I look back.

I tried to be a good child one year in middle school, take basketball, be this super athlete, I was the tallest kid in my class, and people were scared of me and already knew me on the other teams.

I remember coming home with my sister, our door was locked, she slipped her library card and opened the door, fucking worse thing she could ever show me. From that day on I knew how to break into people's homes. That's why we got evicted because I started robbing people's homes when I was eleven. The way I got caught my little pack they're younger than me. I was trying to be this super fuck-the-world whatever, because I wasn't going to heaven anyway I was this gay kid, gay people find soul mates in jail and shit; you know there's gonna be this butch ass woman you'll be bestfriends with, and that's what I thought then, like super crazy.

---

1 A forty-ounce bottle of beer.

I used to rob my friends, they were Korean, they had more than me, and I was like, 'Fuck.' They went out on a camping trip, that fucking house was mine the whole fucking weekend, I was eating their food, taking their videos, taking all the random ass money they left home. And I'd go buy dinner for my family, it was a big ass deal to take the family out for pizza, but there were no questions asked.

But there was this one house I hit, I see my friend's mom go to the Laundromat, I hella run to her house, break in their house, and I take her purse. They worked at the flea market and in her purse there's more than a thousand dollars, and I'm eleven, and I have cash. It changed my life so quick, I'm running down to my house, fucking have all this money for a little ass kid.

I tell my pack, the poorest kids in the complex, my little brother, I gave him fifteen dollars told him to keep his mouth shut, wait for a week, don't spend your money now. I had this motto, Think with your head and not with your heart. I'm completely different now that I'm grown. Yeah my little brother tells the janitor he'll buy him a soda, a little eight-year-old telling this grown ass man he'd buy him a soda. The janitor says, 'Hey, where you getting all your money from?' He says, 'My sister found a purse.' They bring a fricking cop. Handcuff me to a desk. Another kid in the pack tells me he's been to juvenile says he's a hard core thug, he comes out crying, white kid, just saw him recently, just came out of prison. Shocking to me, he went to prison. But after that we were evicted.

My parents were going through a divorce; they were figuring out their situation at that time, there was domestic violence going on that time. My sister came home, Mom was like beating her, like one of those old school beatings; I think she beat us because she was in an abusive relationship with my father. That was why I didn't like my mom when I was younger because of the way she used to beat us. It was like she was trying to take out her anger on us because she was getting beat. I didn't understand that until I got older, I was never in the house, I was outside that day. So my sisters got it, when I got home they said like, 'Hey,' then I knew.

I was on the basketball court and my dad ran out of the house, very panicky. So I go with him in the car ask him where he's going. He told me he was going to buy bread. He always buys a loaf of French bread because it reminds him of home. He's hella asking me questions in Samoan in the car while we drive to Safeway, 'Should I go back?' Pulls out his wallet, because he knows he's going to be arrested, gives me all his money it's like forty dollars. Tells me to take care of my sisters and brother. Then we drive back to the apartment complex, there's fucking cops, the whole neighborhood's outside, because hella cops are there all the time, there's a lot of crime. A lot of people had domestic violence issues there; it's my mom outside she's crying and stuff. He gets out and they arrest my dad, everyone knew my mom got beaten up by my dad; she climbed over the fence told the neighbor. My dad went to jail. I still hated my mom at the time, because she used to beat us and my father not so much. I didn't understand her abuse though, her family always hated my dad; later in life I understood, and I tried to understand why he was an abuser. I went to his domestic violence classes with him. I try to figure it out every day.

I was incarcerated once and my brother wrote me he was very supportive he accepted my queerness before I accepted it; he always wanted to be like me. I remember we were young it was Halloween he was like, you should wear a suit and I will wear a dress, and he won the costume contest. He's a big ass macho guy, 6'4 solid with tattoos and he was only 14. He's the guy everyone wants to be around because he's a cool dude. And I felt he did that then because he just wanted to support me, because he always knew I never wanted to wear a dress. I hella cried about that, I don't want to wear this shit! I used to be hella embarrassed, ran into the house right away coming home from church, wore basketball shorts under my dress, changed in the van and came out. And then he wrote me when I was incarcerated, said, I'm glad that you're gay, a lot of people don't know this but I'm half gay. He was, probably, more queer friendly than I was; but I was hella homophobic, fucking gay people, trying to hide my gayness, I'd be like, 'Oh, your dyke ass friend there.' Hella condescending.

I was a good student, I was the fastest reader, I hella loved reading. I think I thought too much, it was because I was queer, I guarantee you I had to think in my head. I had a crush on my kindergarten teacher; she was fucking fly. How do you tell your grown ass teacher? I'd hella wait until she hugged me. In elementary school I remember my first crush, she was Hawaiian, she was hella fly. I thought, 'Should I wear my hat this way; should I wear a hat?' I thought, 'Maybe she'll like me if I act like a boy.'

Sometimes I don't feel really butch but it's kinda obvious I'm super masculine. I see a lot of lesbian women that really try super hard, I know internally they're very masculine centered people, the only way that they feel they can express their masculinity is through their physical, sometimes their body can reject that unless they're taking some kind of drugs or whatever. When I see women that are butch, I'm like fuck, I don't really have to do shit, I was born with broad ass shoulders, flat chested. They have to put in a lot of effort, they're always trying to get big; they're, 'What do you do, you work out?' I'm like, 'Naw, I lift laundry, I lift boxes,' it's very Samoan to be masculine, a natural masculinity that has femininity.

When I was like thirteen, I was like, 'Fuck, maybe I should date a guy,' my best friend Tubbs who knew I was queer, laughed, only time I tried. He was joking, 'Wouldn't it be weird if we dated?' I was like, 'Eww that's fucking gross.' He said, 'I know it is fucking gross it would be like dating a dude, I would be gay, but you're gay.' That was the first time someone said I was gay, he just knew.

My first woman was when I was sixteen, she was twenty-four. I thought I was never coming out. So I never really took shit seriously. When I was older I began doing random community organising, I always saw queer people in the social justice community and college people in anything social justice. I was like, 'Fuck, there's one day when I'm gonna have to.' I was learning about women of color issues of being poor; queerness would never have to come up. To me being gay was such a heterosexual way of thinking of masculinity and patriarchy, you're a man and that's a woman whatever.

I don't think I was very attracted to the idea of being gay, that just meant you're having sex with the same sex and there's nothing more to it. It would just be a heterosexual relationship with a woman and you play the man. I'm queer in every aspect, being poor whatever, my relationships could grow more than something that people perceived, my understanding of gay and queerness, it's very hard to explain. When I was young I'm going to date the femmiest whatever, I'm going to be the man, it was the phoniest shit I could ever think of, it was a marketed dream to have a normal life like that, then I realised I would never have that kind of normal life in America because I'm not straight.

I used to treat women like shit, like, 'Bitch', 'Ho', whatever, it was easier to be like that because my family they're used to these heterosexual relationships where people treat each other like that in the hood. It's hella complicated for me to explain to my younger cousin, what queer means, it's a privileged word to use, very academic, there has to be another word than queer, it could be a Samoan word like ufalele.[2] It has to do with every aspect of my life not just who I sleep with.

I remember Shawanda, the first lesbian I seen in my life, she was black and she was a stud, her girlfriend was Native American, the finest fucking girl you ever seen in your life. I hella admired her when I was super young, this woman Shawanda in our neighborhood. There was a woman at church too, she played drums and obviously she was hella gay. But I couldn't get into a conversation; now I can get into a conversation on this with my family.

I grew up with people laughing all the time, 'Oh here comes', and laughing. I was like, 'Fuck that guy, I don't want to be gay'. I'd hella pray, 'Please make me a man or un-gay me cuz I can't do this shit'. Even though I never really wanted to be a man. Now

---

2 Fly ass.

I see these kids they're super comfortable with their sexuality, people who are comfortable with themselves they provide that space for those kids so it's safe. Being poor, being a criminal, it was very easy for me to stick with those identities rather than another one. That life is over a long time, since the last time I was incarcerated.

There was a point where it was pointed in a direction where I had no control. I was related to the hoodest Samoan family; my cousin was a super drug dealer. I tried to go to college but in my family no one even thinks about college or the future in that way. I didn't know what the fuck to do with my life, I was a smart kid, and I lived a double life, I'd dip in and I'd dip out when I wanted to. I went to jail and graduated from high school two weeks later. It was robbery; we'd steal stock from the pharmacy, repackage and sell it back to the pharmacy; hella random ass shit. The cops wanted me to snitch on all these people; I didn't do it.

Money was so crazy back then. I would have so much money and be miserable and not know what to do with my money because I was used to not paying for shit. I was like a very miserable person with lots of money, in high school. I have a bad relationship with money now because I'm not that person now. I'm in a gray place with money now, not a capitalist, but I have all I need and that's it.

I went to college, couldn't finish because I got locked up again, but I'll go back. I turned twenty-one, in jail; I had my birthday there. It was cute. I had the greatest experience in jail; I went in there with a different mindset. You realise these women they're mothers, they're sisters, it was me coming to grips with my queerness, understanding women in a different way than how I always looked at women in a very patriarchal way. You'll never hear a woman's story who's incarcerated, fucking crazy ass story, being oppressed by men, what happens to their children, I'd hella talk to these women, they thought I was a snitch but I was genuinely curious. They'd call me Dr. Phil. It made me have the most respect I could ever have for a woman, being incarcerated, these were mothers who were once raped, people abused these women, all they wanted was to be with their children. Their children may not love them. Their children lives to be better was their dream. Their stories will never be told because they don't get the opportunity or have the resources.

Sometimes people take on stereotypes, especially men. I think that men are more egotistical than women. Sometimes men like to live up to these stereotypes. I have a cousin he's super flamboyant, in front of me he's quiet. You don't have to put that on for me. Sometimes I think lesbians and Samoans are socially awkward in America, this is what I find. I think because a lot of them don't know the language to express themselves, don't know how to explain fa`a Sāmoa to their teachers. I taught a workshop in the East Palo Alto,[3] one of the girls told me that that was the first time she learned anything in her own entire school year about being Samoan when I taught there because these American teachers don't know how to speak to them.

Now I teach kids media through their social biography here at Silicon Valley De-Bug. That organisation saved my life. The reason why it's named De-Bug, everyone thinks that's a software company, it's in the Silicon Valley where people has this misconception it's rich people because the dot com burst, Google, Yahoo, EBay, millionaires and billionaires who live in the Silicon Valley beside the people who clean their homes and take care of their children. There was a floor of temp workers called the De-Bug Unit. When the people on the top couldn't figure out what was wrong with the motherboard they'd send it down for people to find the problem, expose it and find the solution, that's why De-Bug is called debug. It's a community organisation, we work on social justice, we do a lot of legal work for free, pro bono legal work, photography, teach kids media, teach workshops, we have a website, come out with a magazine. When we do media people have to write their own script. Our saying is, 'Experience is the ultimate authority.' I'm just an editor; I make it sound pretty.

---

3   East Palo Alto, near San Jose, California.

I would always laugh at activists, it was these college kids who were hella like obsessed with struggle, I'm like, 'Fuck dude I'm right here what the fuck!' They didn't like me because I didn't read Malcolm X's autobiography, couldn't talk about that, but I could tell you how to rob a house, they were like, 'Fuck, I don't want to hang out with you.' They were kinda scared, I always think it's like you're scared of the truth. You can't teach struggle in an institution, it's something you feel.

I'm going back to college next year; I'm going to be a super fucking nerd. I used to love going to college, they'd look at me like some thug ass guy, my teacher used to read my essays to piss off the other students because she didn't like those students, she'd be, 'Thank you Jean thank you.' I went to Atlanta for the Social Forum, a networking thing for activists, but it was crazy, I thought maybe the people of the city should know about it. I was hanging with these Blood gangs in Atlanta, hella nice ass guys, 'Hey do you know about the Social Forum?' They were, 'What the fuck is that?' People were scared to talk to them, people who lived that reality.

Went to an after-party, almost died, can't control what I say sometimes, I come outside, see my friend Erica who I'm in OLO, One Love Oceania[4] Pasifika queer women's group with. All I hear is some guys say, 'Bitch!' to Erica. I'm like, 'Oh my god did this guy just call my friend a bitch?' I'm like, 'What'd you say? Come over here, you'd better apologise.'

He's from Atlanta, he said, 'What the fuck! Who the hell are you?' We're about to get in this big ass scuffle; they're trying to push me back into the club.

I'm like, 'What? Get out of here; you can't even get in the club with your Target bag.' He was holding this Target shopping bag, who the fuck comes to the club with a Target shopping bag? He was talking about how he was going to kill me, and all this shit. He was wearing this gold Jesus piece. 'How the fuck are you going to take my life and you have a Jesus piece on?'

---

4 Queer Pacific women's poetry group in San Francisco Bay Area.

He left, I think he was going to go get something. My friends throw me in a cab, we go down the street, and fucking we stop at the stop sign. To the left, this fucking white guy is getting robbed by all these dope fiends. This guy screams, 'Help!' Fifteen dope fiends on this white guy. So we grab him, we get out. We're supposed to go to these activist workshops, were hanging out with these Bloods, getting a tour guide by their little sister her name was Muffin, we learn the Superman, this dance they were all doing in sync. Most of the people from OLO were there, beautiful women in social justice, like Fui and Loa Niumeitolu.

We were like, we should make a queer Pacific Islander women's group, we were drinking, and it's like a kava session. One Love Oceania, Epeli Hau`ofa's idea we're all connected. And then OLO happened. We marched in the Dyke March. Hella lot of white lesbians treated me like shit, thought I was a Pacific Islander man. OLO molded me in my queer destiny.

OLO hella pushed me to become an artist. Art is such a booty call for me; I only use it when I go through shit. When I was young I always wrote and it was only because I went through hella shit, it'd be an outlet and then I'd throw it away. After I would feel better, I'd be, 'Okay, I'm cool,' and then move on with my life. It was like a booty call, you'd call someone and say, 'Hey, come make me feel good, because I feel like shit right now,' and then you'd throw them away. I'm trying to build my relationship with art. And through OLO, I guess it's okay to be an artist.

I just did a mixed media mural, photography and painting exhibition, it was fun. My family ended up doing most of the painting, and it was the most beautiful thing that could ever happen, working together on this gay ass mural. My family is from Hunters Point, so these kids from the projects, nothing could replace that, my time with my family, my friends helping me paint a queer Samoan mural. Hella loved that mural. The Samoan Community Development Center, I brought some of the kids there, first art show they've ever been to. To me, ah, that was it.

Sal Salamaotua Tatupu Poloai

Growing up in L.A. most Sals are Mexican, but my dad wanting to give me an American name I became Sal Salamaotua. Poloai is a matai name that my dad has; he was a high talking chief. But I'm more of a mama's boy than a daddy's son. I was at one time the only son. My dad is a very short man, I'm 6′ 2″ so I get my height from my mom's side, her brothers are like 6′ 5″, 6′ 8″, tall guys. My dad's a very quiet man. He's a blue-collar man, loved cricket, loved beer, worked hard, very quiet and humble man, totally the opposite from me, he's quiet I'm not, he's very reserved I'm very loud. When he walks in a room he's the kind of person that walks towards the side, whereas me I have to walk in with a grand entrance and let everyone know that I'm here.

My mom and me are kinda like that. She used to wear, this is in the seventies, you remember, people used to wear those beehive buns; well, hers is over the top. She's like, Wow! all the other women be looking at her, and me when I go in people will know that I walked in. Her name is Milaneta Mamea from `Aoa.[1] They both passed, my mom in 1976 and my dad in 2007. I'm forty-six young, was born in Honolulu, but all my life was in L.A. Started off in Carson, on Marbella; after my mom passed we moved to Gardena, a lot of Japanese Americans, mixed neighborhood, very diverse. We were Methodist, Mila's church,[2] we went there.

I was like any typical kid living in Carson[3] until twelve. Did everything, baseball, football. My first experience with a guy was at twelve, I still remember, Victor, this guy was Mexican, an

---

1 Village and bay on northeast shore of Tutuila Island, American Sāmoa.
2 Samoan Methodist church in Wilmington in the Los Angeles Harbor area.
3 Suburban city between South Central Los Angeles and the Harbor area.

empty house on Marbella, found a couple nude magazines, 'Hey, can you do what she's doing to me?'

When you're a kid you think, Wow huge houses, but now you go back you think these are small ass houses. There wasn't a whole lot of Samoans in the seventies, on our block maybe three families; now the whole block's Samoan. It was in the late seventies. A whole lot of Samoans came down. Carson exploded in the late seventies.

Hip hop started in the early eighties, '81: Grandmaster Flash, Run DMC. The Boo-Yaa T.R.I.B.E.,[4] I went to school with them, very academically not inclined, and he led his big family of brothers. They had their own following, it started as a dance group, remember in the seventies they had pop locking, black and Filipino dance groups, then rapping, and Boo-Yaa became big.

Gangs started around that time too. I only knew one Samoan gang at that time, Samoan Liberation Army, SLA. Then from there grew out to be CSW, Carson Samoan Warriors, after the movie *Warriors* came out, and then you had SOS, Sons of Sāmoa. And in Compton you had Park Village, only really poor Samoan people lived in Park Village.

They're not like the typical gangs you see where they have territory, Mexicans usually they'll own blocks within a city, blacks are the same way, and they're usually named after streets. Samoans is a different type, I always think Samoan gangs start off from churches because they all came from the same church, they came from all over the place, you know, Samoans don't live in like one area, but there's one place they all congregate at church. I didn't really get into gangs but everybody hung out with each other. Whether it was just a way to have a group I don't know, was never involved.

Peary Junior High was not so far from Joey's Billiards,[5] I used

---

4 First well-known Samoan rap crew and hip-hop band from Carson, L.A.

5 Samoan and Chicano bar in Carson in the seventies.

Sal Salamaotua Tatupu Poloai
Photograph: Courtesy of contributor

to sneak in, and I was always a big kid. As soon as you walk in you have about six tall standing tables, he had like three pool tables in the middle, the bar, tons of Sams, tons of low-riders, your typical dive bar filled with a bunch of ethnic people, cheap drinks, quarts of beer for fifty cents back then. Samoans were Sams, now they're Hamos, now they're uzs [bros] I guess.

I'd just hang out with people. The only reason I hung out with the older guys ten or twenty years older than I am, they had money, they were buying. No girls. If they came by it was to pick them up, bring food whatever. The only reason the guys would come into the parking lot was to smoke weed or eat pizza or whatever. Your typical saloon, there were always fights; if it wasn't in the pool hall it was in the parking lot.

These were the first generation of Samoans born in the States; spoke English. There was a different group of Samoans who spoke Samoan hung out at the Lariat, that's where my dad would hang out, or the older – my dad's generation would hang out at the Tiki. When I moved to Gardena I started going to other places where Samoans weren't going to, these were places in Santa Monica, Westwood and West Hollywood.[6]

My mom was a fag hag, had a fa`afafine friend Michelle, she lived in Carson, went to Dominguez,[7] they'd do all these sewing and stuff. Michelle was always loud, very flamboyant, very out there, funny. Every time I'd see Michelle she'd have a `ie lavalava tied around her breast, almost walking around half naked half her life, she was just a very flamboyant person who was very happy. The other one was Ane Iopo, he was gay, went to church together, older, another one of my mom's friends.

I was close with them but it was more the fear of coming out, being the only son – my dad was mister cricket player, so I didn't want to come out, I was too afraid. Every time it was like, 'You are a disappointment.' He played piano, I didn't. He played sports, I did; that's why I played football, that's why every time

---

6 Where many L.A. gay bars were in the seventies and still are.
7 California State University Dominguez Hills in Carson.

we had a game against Carson or Banning,[8] he'd sit on the other side bleachers cheering on because all the Samoan kids come from there. I was like, Oh God. He's a very hard man to please. I gave up and said, 'Oh, forget it.'

I began hanging out at the Rage, the Dungeon when I was going to Santa Monica, you go to these places and they've got four stories of dance floor, it was crazy. I went with girls, danced, got high, and got drunk.

Gardena, typical, I was very masculine, played football. Actually that's how I got my scholarship to go to school, was playing football. I went to Gardena, from there went to Santa Monica, then Prairie View A&M, about forty-five minutes outside of Houston, it's an all black university. I never saw so many black people. We played in New Orleans the Superdome, I'd see eighty thousand black people. It's a different culture for them.

When I moved to Gardena, being the only Samoan in the high school and you've got all these different ethnic groups, different cliques, I couldn't really fit in to any one of them, so I basically just made friends with all of them. In Prairie View it's easier that way, too, you've got a great diversity of black people. You get blacks that are from the country, blacks that are from the city. So we had guys from Chicago and New York, Philadelphia, L.A., San Francisco. Then you had those blacks that were from, like, Cut-and-Shoot Texas, or Mississippi, or Tennessee. Then you've got the light-skinned blacks that are Creole. Then you have what they like to call the dark chocolate black.

They thought I was black Native American French, I was like, 'No, I'm Samoan.' They're like, 'What's that?' 'They're like Hawaiians.' In front of the geography class there's this huge map of the world, the professor asks everyone to put a pin into where your ancestors are from. Me, I've never been to Sāmoa before, I don't know where the hell it's at in the Pacific. I can see Hawai`i;

---

8 Carson High School in Carson and Banning High School in Wilmington.

it has to be near Hawaii somewhere. The professor knew where I was from, served here during World War II, says, 'You're here', and moves the pen all the way down, 'You're here'.

At Prairie View I had a girlfriend, she was more of a stalker than anything else, basically I kept her around because everyone said, 'Oh, you don't have a girl, you don't have a girl?' Most of my time was partying, having fun with people, I really didn't do anything sexual, my mind wasn't on it, but this girl kept coming round, I kept her around as more of a trophy than anything else, she was from Louisiana, light-skinned, she'd follow me to the games.

Had one affair, middle line backer, white boy, we were both drunk, he started touching, then it just went on, just once, we'd see each other in the shower … I liked white guys but – and he was a country boy – I had a lot of feelings, didn't know if I wanted to act on them with him. Typical defensive asshole, loud – defense people are very loud, obnoxious, it's part of their psychology, they talk shit, scream at you, talk about your mother, call you a little slut or whatever, most of defensive players are like that. I was an offensive guard – they're quiet, reserved, because we're more trying to figure out how to get our runner from here to there; you're always thinking. I loved the sport, I love the sport, and I'm a diehard Raiders fan.

But it was from Texas, in 1987, my dad decided to retire, move back here [to American Sāmoa], take on his chief titles and all that stuff. I was twenty-two. I didn't finish college, I was a junior, had a scholarship but my father decided I'd move back: I was the only child, he's moving, he's going back by himself, he came back to get married. Samoan people, we have this loyalty to our parents, no matter how old you get we have this loyalty, the integrity, there's that issue – when your parents ask you something in our culture, you go, there's no ifs, ands or buts, you just drop, go.

Hawaiian Air, it was an old ass plane, I thought what am I getting into, once the plane lands the stewardess goes around spraying this fog thing. Got off, it's the first time I actually had to walk down the stairs, it was very dark, they open that door, there's this rush of hot humid air on my face, I still remember, I think, I'm in deep shit. What the hell am I doing, my God, you see people in the distance they're waving. The only person I know is my dad. He tells me there's someone going to be there to pick me up. Hundreds of people standing there staring at me, my dad's sister with her kids and ten other kids to pick up one person, old Toyota pickup trunk with a tarp over it, I'm sitting in the back of a pickup truck thinking oh my God this is so fucking ghetto. I think, I'm dying I'm dying. Soon as you passed the airport, darkness, couldn't see your hand in front of you. I'm thinking, Oh shit we're in the jungle now, we're actually living in a jungle.

I wake up in the morning to the sounds of roosters and pigs outside the window; I get slapped by a bunch of mosquitoes. My whole intention was to set him up and leave, but he paid for a one-way ticket: I wasn't going to go back to Texas. I ended up staying here; I've been here ever since.

I was leading the fast life in Texas, I was young, we were partying, I'm like, the world is mine, and then I come here it was like a time warp to the Stone Ages. But probably it was a mixed blessing too; my father said, 'You need to slow down.' I got hired as a teacher; they wanted me to teach English because I spoke English. I started teaching; I fell in love with it. Being a teacher you're going to be broke, but my mom wanted me to be a teacher, the irony of it. I got married about six years later.

I only had two brief male experiences here, okay, bite me. Because here everyone is so related to each other. Mentally I fixated myself: never go out with a Samoan. People gossip here bigtime. I won't do it with another Samoan – the fear of running into a cousin. Maybe if you're afakasi your blood is diluted, I don't know, I never do it here.

I'm the family secretary for my family; I'm the treasurer keeping the genealogy of people who come to fa`alavelave, different types of fa`alavelave, family helping each other. The talking chief and the high chief that are there, they expect the secretary to know all this stuff, who brought what fine mat, they'll say, who brought the ufita`i, who brought the `afuelo, I document that stuff. My Samoan speaking is very limited; the only time I speak is when they ask me questions.

I met my wife at a church in Leone, she's decorating a wedding, I was sitting there, she kept looking, I said hi, hi; went to the reception she's there again, started asking me to dance with her, called me, I'd call her, went out with, you know, with other people, three years later she asked me to marry her. I was lonely, she was lonely, and basically that's what it was. I had my own place. I'm a very independent person. She asked, and I said, 'Yeah.' We were best friends, she's a very family-oriented person, and takes care of the family, her mother. We were together seventeen years. It was lonely still, there was something missing, the first five years was pretty good, we've grown our family, literally nine months after we got married we had our first daughter. Pretty good because the girls were there. First three were all a year apart, now eighteen, seventeen, and sixteen. We took a break, then the fourteen, twelve, and seven-year-olds. Those are my girls; those are the ones that kept me busy.

I don't go out that much here. I'd go off by myself traveling. As soon as I hit Hawai`i I'm a different person. I get off, jump in the cab, and then, it's party time. They know me at Hula's, just Sal; sometimes they call me Yogi Bear – why everyone calls me a fricking bear? I'm not hairy. Everyone in Hawai`i knows, I'd get away six to eight times a year. My job took me to meetings, conferences on education. Then I go off-island – Washington DC, in Alexandria, Virginia, St Louis, Chicago, Las Vegas is also fun.

I go to Hawai`i. I go to Hula's, all the bartenders there, that's who I hang out with, best place to go in Waikiki – cheap drinks, nice sun, Diamond Head. I'm doing New Years Eve at Hula's, those guys are fun, I'll drink all night and my tab will be like seven dollars. Go to Bacchus, Hunters, Tacos, and then you've got Badgers. I go, Badger, is that really your name? he goes, Yeah, and I go, What, Badger in bed or Badger when you were born?

I don't do the clubbing scene so much anymore, like Fusions, Club Seven. Football players are nice eye-candy but I'm attracted to femme guys. The word fa`afafine, that word I identify as someone who wants to be a woman. Why can't I be a man who likes men? Man to man. Hula's, you get a lot of men talking basketball, football, you wouldn't know they're gay.

It took the death of my father to get me to look at myself. It wasn't until he died that he told me. I was here. My dad was on dialysis for a long time. In 2006 the doctors here couldn't do anything else. He was scared, he asked me to take him to California, and I paid for everything, set up all his doctor appointments with my sister. A year later I get a phone call on a Wednesday and he asked me to come, asked me to fly from American Sāmoa to Long Beach like, tomorrow. I knew he was probably getting ready to go. Flew out on a Thursday, came to the hospital Friday, he looks up, says, Get some rest come back in the morning. Saturday got there a little bit after seven, Long Beach Memorial. I look, he's getting ready to go, I knew he was going – I could see it in his eyes. He said he was proud … He died when we left the room, didn't want to in front of us. That was my dad.

Yes, it took the death of my father to get me to look at myself. I was pushing four hundred pounds, being married, sitting behind a desk, eating all the time, and smoking. Both my parents died from diabetes, my dad was on dialysis, my mom died from insulin shock. I thought, Wow, my kids are young, I better take care of myself. Changed my diet, began walking six to eight miles a day, I'm down to two-sixty, twenty-five to go, also work out at the gym, try and hold everything together, I call it weight reassignment, try and move whatever's down here to somewhere else.

After my girls were grown I'd work ten to twelve hour days, six, seven days a week, keeping busy, nothing to do here, work was a way of occupying my time. Social life was zero. I wouldn't see my wife until ten, eleven o'clock for one or two hours … That went on for seventeen years, that was our relationship, one or two hours. It wasn't until she began to realise, I came out to her about three years ago, I told her, 'There's something missing in our relationship and I just feel blank.' She started trying to get more physical. I said, 'It's not this, it's more emotional ... we're still friends, [but] there's this part you can't fulfill, you're just not able to.' I'm trying to explain to her these things but it's a shock for her. She's thinking that I'm leaving her for a man, and that's embarrassing; that gay is wrong. She even started hunting down my family and telling them, 'Talk to him, he's wrong, he's going to go to Hell.' Even my uncle was telling me I'm going to Hell with what I'm doing, I go, 'Well, you know what, I like warm places.'

It was harder for her than it was for me. I finally came to a decision, 'Okay, I'm getting old, the girls are here, that part's complete, but there's still something missing.' My daughters, that was hard, but they accepted it. Brought them down, sat them down in a room in Pavaiai, and just told them, 'I want you guys to hear this from me before you hear it from other people.' Explained to them, basically told them, 'Do you know what gay is?' The older ones knew. 'What does it mean?' 'You know, when a guy likes a guy or a girl likes a girl.' 'Do you guys think it's wrong?' 'No.' 'Do you think it's wrong if I say your dad's gay?' They go, 'We kinda knew.' They already knew.

'We knew you were having problems with Mom but we also knew that, you know, sometimes you walk around – you know. You were the one who taught us how to bake a cake and do cookies; what dad does that?' So they accepted it. Yesterday we spent all day Christmas shopping. My girls understand, they know. The younger ones, they're still young. I live in Pavaiai, and their mom and the girls live in the house I built for them on their mother's family property in Leone.

There's an issue of being closeted and coming out. I hear it all the time from people, 'How can you do that to your kids?' 'What am I doing to my kids? If anything I'm telling them how to speak the truth, my kids accepted it, so get over it.'

A marriage is really about two people that want to commit

to one another, that love one another, and whether those two individuals are a man and a woman, a man and a man, or a woman and a woman shouldn't really matter, these are two people who want to commit to one another, and they should be allowed to marry. Sāmoa, that issue hasn't really come up here, I know a lot of men here who live together who are not married, recognised by the government. All these guys, they pay taxes; if something happens to them their partner will not be taken care of.

Catholicism practices, preaches how gay is not accepted, and the Anglican or Kaiki[9] churches, but yet you go to any of these congregations, there are about ten, fifteen gay guys and women that are recognised, everybody knows that they're gay, sitting in the church. They're transgender, cross dressers, some of them are just femme guys, but they're gay, and everybody knows, and they're sitting in a church that preaches against gays.

SOFIAS, one of the organisations here for fa`afafines, they do a pageant here every year, and the money that they raise goes to Fatuaiga for the elderly, and Fatuaiga is run by the Catholic Church that basically says, Oh, gay is wrong but they're taking money from a group of gay people. So, how can you on one side of the coin say, gay is bad, but with the other hand accept the money that's from a gay person? These are big issues, they're national issues, global issues. Sāmoa is going to have to ask itself, How do we want to see our people? As a culture we accept fafa things, so why can't we do it as a government?

It's been a rollercoaster ride since I came out to my wife because she then outed me to the rest of the community; her and her sisters went and told everybody. I go, she's very angry, rightfully she should be, and she probably feels like she's been cheated. I accept it, I won't be mad at her, she's human. People talk, we work on a small college campus where I'm the dean, but it's my performance that basically keeps their mouth shut. You

---

9 Loku Kaiki or Lotu Taiti church, the London Missionary Society-originated Samoan Congregational Church, which came to Sāmoa from Kaiki/Taiti or Tahiti.

can talk the talk but if you can't walk the walk get the hell out of my way.

I'm more looking [out] for my girls; I want to get them a house in Hawai`i so they can continue their education there. My oldest girl wants to be a nurse, the second one wants to be an international lawyer, I have to figure out where they'll be staying; waiting for my girls to leave ASCC[10] and come out to Hawai`i. I have a Masters in Instructional Technology. A lot of people want me to work on my PhD.

I gotta go to class; hey, class is done, let's go to Hula's. It's been a journey for me. Once you're out it's like this whole world was lifted off your shoulders. I can walk around, tell people I'm gay and not even worry about it. Last night I was at Tradewinds where there's a lot of politicians and businesspeople that hang out there that think they're big shots, and then in walks this 6′ 2″, 260-pound gay man, that they still have to humble themselves down because they know he's a power player. So just be honest to yourself and accept it. And everything will be all right.

---

10   American Sāmoa Community College.

Kiana Rivera

Puzzy

by Kiki
featuring Victor Rodger[1]

Synopsis

Mele, a lesbian Samoan Jehovah's Witness, struggles with her sexuality and her quest for true love.

Characters

Actor One: Mele, played by Frankie Adams
Actor Two: Tina Turner, Persis, Auntie Momi, Michael (and others), played by Nora Koloi
Actor Three: Queen Kanutri (and others), played by Malia Ahovelo
Actor Four: Elder John, Grandma Lola, Gina Davis (and others), played by Gabs Solomona

---

1 Puzzy is by Kiki (Kiana Rivera), featuring New Zealand Samoan fa`afafine playwright Victor Rodger. With special thanks to mana wahine Fata Simanu-Klutz and Tagi Qolouvaki for lending their voices to the script. Puzzy made its world premiere at the Auckland Pride Festival on February 9, 2016 under the direction of Anapela Polataivao.

#1: MELE and her INNER DEMONS

INNER DEMON #1: Are you gay?

INNER DEMON #2: Are you straight?

INNER DEMON #3: What are you? Bi or bicurious?

INNER DEMON #1: Lesbian?

INNNER DEMON #2: Queer?

INNER DEMON #3: Dyke?

INNER DEMON #1: Pretty boi?

INNER DEMON #2: Trans?

INNER DEMON #3: Pussy lover.

INNER DEMON #1: Pussy muncher.

INNER DEMON #2: Munch.

INNER DEMON #3: Munch her!

ALL: What are you?

MELE: I don't know! I'm neither! I'm either! I'm all of them. I'm none of them.

 The girls begin to chant: 'CHOOSE, choose, choose, choose ...'

INNER DEMON #1: Choose!

MELE: I'm ... I'm gay. Why can't that be enough?

INNER DEMON #2: It's never enough!

MELE: I'm ... I'm bi?

INNER DEMON #3: Choose!

MELE: I'm a lesbian?

INNER DEMON #1: Choose!

Kiana Rivera
Photographer: Slava Slavik

MELE: No. I'm ...

INNER DEMON #2: Choose!

MELE: I'm me. I'm MELE. I'm Samoan. I'm Filipino. I'm a Jehovah's Witness.

INNER DEMON #3: Choose!

MELE: I'm ... gay. I'm sexually fluid.

INNER DEMON #1: Choose!

MELE: I'm all of them. But just a little bit of all of them. I'm me. Actually I don't fucking know who I am. I don't know what I am.

ALL: CHOOSE!

MELE: All I know is that I like pussy.FUCK!

'Pussy' by Iggy Azaela plays.
Everyone walks forward. Looks up, as if they're watching porn.

MELE amongst PUSSY LOVERS

LESBIAN #1: Mm mm mm. My favorite puzzy was sweet, soft and juicy. It was creamy. Caramel creamy. That puzzy cat belonged to a sexy, brown Samoan suga with the sweetest pussy to grace this face. Her lips were thick and always moist.

NORA: My favourite pussy tasted sweet like caramel with a hint of saltiness. Yes, her pussy was salted caramel frappuccino. So snug and warm inside. So pleased to see me, to feel me ... so pleased to have me. Soft, snug, wet, warm, sweet, salty and wanting. Wanting to swallow me whole. And I, wanting to be engulfed by its sweet, warm earthiness, diving deep into a pool of silky brown puzzy liqueur.

MELE: Well, my favourite pussy was ... my favourite pussy was ... actually I don't have that much experience, but there was this one time I was rubbing this girl's clitoris but then I realised it was actually her right labia so she wasn't really having a good time so –

BISCUIT: Fuck, man, pussy makes me poetic and shit! Sometimes I just look into a valley, like with trees and shit and think of pussy. Cuz valleys are deep, mysterious, moist. Damn. So living in Tits – WEST SIDE – I'm thinking about pussy aaaall the fuuuckin time, nigga! Yeahya!

GRANDMA LOLA (Samoan, fresh)

Mele! Oh that girl. She always so busy. She so busy she no got time to find a husband. Eh, she better get married. Have children before she too old. I always pray for her, you know? Ho' boy. Satan is really ruling dis world now. You see they legalise the gays to marry? Oh! So *terrible*. Really show we living in the last days. Dis is when we really need, Jehovah God.
    Amene.

AUNTY MOMI (stoner older Samoan)

You know, you always hear about the fa`afafine, but you don't hear about the fa`afatama.
    You know a fa`afatama because you see the two girl togetha and one only use the lavalava and the other one use the lavalava with the pocket and a T-shirt and they always togethah. All the people in the village know, but no one say a thing, We don't make a deal out of it ah! ia.
    I can't tell which one is Mele, but I fink she is a fafa something.
    That girl is such a good girl. It's okay Mele don't have a boyfriend. But I think Mele is a gay. Kalofae! But we still love Mele. Mele is so sweet,

The girls begin to sing 'Make the Truth Your Own' (JW hymn) ...

MELE and TINA at church

MELE: Yo, Tina: Who's that sister with the curly hair?

TINA: Which one? You mean Vanessa?

MELE: No, not her. The big curly hair. Right there. And the kinda big nose.

TINA: White dress?

MELE: Yeah.

TINA: I dunno. Why?

MELE: What is she? Greek? That looks like a Greek nose. And she's tall and has all that hair.

TINA: Are you a lesbian?

MELE: I'm not a lesbian. Women are better looking than men. That's all. That doesn't make me a lesbo.

MELE laughs hysterically.

ELDER JOHN: Leviticus ch. 18.

'Jehovah continued to speak to Moses, saying: "Speak to the Israelites and say to them, 'I am Jehovah your God. You must not behave as they do in the land of Egypt, where you were dwelling, and you must not do what they do in the land of Canaan, where I am bringing you.'

'You must not lie down with a male in the same way that you lie down with a woman. It is a detesticle act.'

'This goes for women who lie with women.'"'

MELE steps forward.

MELE: (*To God*) I know you're watching me God. I know you know the truth But this is who I am. This is who you've created. If you don't like it, you don't have to watch. But this is me. Sorry.

MELE and VANESSA. Drunk.

MELE: You told them? You really told them?

VANESSA: I've been lying all my life, Mele. I can't do it anymore.

MELE: Once you do this, that's it, Vanessa. You can't talk to anyone. No one can talk to you. You'll be dis-fellowshipped. Out of the organisation. Out of the kingdom!

VANESSA: I don't need the congregation to tell me Jehovah loves me. I know Jehovah loves me.

MELE: Aren't you scared?

VANESSA: Aren't you tired?

MELE: Of what?

VANESSA: The lies.

MELE: ... What lies?

VANESSA: Don't be afraid to say it. It'll be okay.

MELE: If I got dis-fellowshipped it would break Grandma's heart. Maybe even kill her.

VANESSA: No it won't.

MELE: You don't know Grandma, Vanessa.

VANESSA: Good luck, Mele.

MELE and TINA going door to door

TINA: We missed you at bible study last night. Uni must be getting busy.

MELE: Yeah. It is. Plus I'm in a show, *The Most Massive Woman Wins*.

TINA: Is it about a big fat piggy wiggy?

MELE: Actually, it's about body image.

TINA: On my God, BORRRRING! Hey – did you hear about Vanessa? She's a total lesbian. Got dis-fellowshipped. TOTAL SCANDALLLLL.

MELE: Wow.

TINA: Wanna get this one?

MELE: You can get it.

TINA: Don't be scared. You gotta practice. Do it for Jehovah. *(Signals MELE.)* Helllooo!

MELE: Okay, fine. (*Knock, knock.*) Helllooo?

ELDERLY JAPANESE WOMAN: What you want?

MELE: Hi! How are you today? We're Jehovah's Witnesses and we're just in your neighborhood sharing some good news with our neighbors. Do you have a couple minutes?

ELDERLY JAPANESE WOMAN: Fuck off. Jehovah's Witness. Fuckface.

MELE: Um, May Jehovah's holy spirit be with you.

ELDERLY JAPANESE WOMAN: Fuck you.

MELE and TINA play Truth or Dare

TINA: Okay, so, let's play Truth or Dare. You first.

MELE: Okay. Truth.

TINA: Yeah okay, Truth. So are you a lesbian or what?

> *(MELE stares shocked at TINA for a few beats.)*

TINA: I knew it!!

MELE: Um, I didn't say anything!

TINA: Oh my God, I fucking knew it. You kissed girls? Do you eat pussy?!

MELE: Oh my God, can you not ...?

TINA: Just answer the question. Do you eat pussy or not?

MELE: Okay, fine. You want to know if I eat pussy? Alright then. I'm gonna tell you about the first pussy I ate.

TINA: Alright, alright, joke's over now.

MELE: I'm gonna make you squirm like she squirmed!!

TINA: You're so disgusting.

MELE: Damn! That pussy was good.

TINA: Yeah, okay, you've had your little joke now –

MELE: Listen to this: I spread her open with my fingers like this *(demonstrates)* then started licking slooowly from the bottom making my way to the tip top of her ... *(winks)* you know. But I did that to each of her lips. The bottom lips, not the top. After I made her cum from ...

TINA: Will you FUCKING PLEASE JUST FUCKING STOP PLEASE?

MELE: ... from playing and sucking her clit, she was so wet ...

TINA: I'm gonna throw up my Subway meatballs.

MELE: C'mon! I'm not done!

TINA: Yes, you are.

MELE: But I haven't told you about deep sea diving all the way up her cave!

TINA: Ahhhhhhhck! *(makes gagging sounds)*

MELE: PUSSY.

EVERYONE: BEST. THING. EVER!

They repeat this chant twice as they get into formation
for Spoken Word ...

SPOKEN WORD #1 (SANDI)

SANDI: Kia ora wahine toa of Tamaki Makaurau and welcome
to spoken word…for The Lemons.

Play You
Your body is my instrument.
Its beat bounces against my chest and radiates
Down Down Down To my
Feet/PUSSY
My fingers
Pressed against your smooth ivory Keys.
The weight of my fingers strike a chord that resounds
Producing a wave of … ohhh …
My lips to your laughter, An a cappella for my soul. My lips
To your flute I blow.
My blow Produces A sound So deep
Vibrations go Down
Down Down To your
Feet/PUSSY Our drums beat
Deep, bump Deep, bump Deep, bump Bump, deep.
I bathe in your sweet Sweet music
Make me weak. Make me need More
Music.

The others click their fingers.

TINA and MELE at a gay club

TINA: Black mini skirt and tube top. She's cute. I can see you
with her.

MELE: She's alright.

TINA: What kinda girls do you like anyway? Do you have a type?

MELE: Yeah. Hot.

TINA: Yeah. Hot with a wet pussy!

MELE: Yes, with a wet pussy! And they have to be able to hold a conversation. Can't have a wet pussy and a dried brain.

TINA: So does that mean you're a butch? A boi? A pretty boi dyke?

MELE: Can't I just be gay?

TINA: There's categories, aren't there? Like gay boys are either tops or bottoms. Do women have the same? I mean, you look like a lipstick, so does that mean you're a lipstick who likes other lipsticks?

MELE: *(puzzled)* I have no idea. This is all new to me.

TINA: Oh my gawd, that's Dana from Congregation? OMG! I didn't know she was like that!!

MELE: That's her wife over there in blue. I heard they're trying to have a baby.

TINA: Hey do you think that butchie will buy me a drink?

Without waiting for a response, TINA goes over to a butch lesbian and does a sexy dance.

She comes back with a drink.

MELE: I can't believe you just flirted with a lesbian to get a drink.

TINA: It's just a drink. I'd do it at a regular club.

MELE: But this is a gay club!

TINA: A free drink is a free drink.

'Sorry' by Justin Bieber comes on.

TINA: Oh my Gooooood, damn, nigga, they're playing my jam!

The girls all do Parris Goebel's choreography from 'Sorry'.

SPOKEN WORD #2 (BISCUIT)

BISCUIT:

Brown Masterpiece

I was caught swimming in your masterpiece. You opened up
  your worlds to me, your layers.

I swam deeper, deeper until I reached depths unknown. The
  water got thick the farther down I swam.

I reached another world. Your world

Warmer, darker, full of soul

A soul seldom touched, seldom seen.

The girls laugh.

BISCUIT:

Fuck up please.

Brown.

Your soul is brown.

A silky, soft, blanket of brown. Swimming in a soul of brown.

The color of caramel, the color of sugar, the color of …

TINA: Shit.

BISCUIT: Fuck up, cunt.

Beat.

BISCUIT:

The color of you.

Waves.

Rolling waves, actively pushing me out of your sea

toward the shore; the curvilinear lines where elements kiss,
  the shore where I once entered

your masterpiece.

The others click their fingers.

MELE and TINA on their lunch break.

MELE: So how was your date?

TINA: OH MY GOSH! So, we go to the club and ALL his friends were there! Waiting for him! He left me to go kick it with his boys all night then I had to drive him and his drunk friends to KFC where he expected ME TO PAY!

MELE: *(laughing)* I guess your South Pacific fantasy is gonna stay just that.

TINA: Shattered dreams cuz. Shattered dreams.

MELE: That's what happens when you date Polynesians. Hello?

TINA: So did you find a hot girl in the end!?

MELE: I never told you about Persis? 'The Indian'?

TINA: Ohh, Indian women are gorgeous.

MELE: That was some Kamasutra shit, right there.

MELE and PERSIS the INDIAN fuck

MELE: Mmmmm. You like that?

PERSIS: Ohhh yeah. Open me up. Uuuhhhh

MELE: Are you OK?

PERSIS: Yes! Yes! Don't stop.

MELE: Sorry. Mmmmmm

PERSIS: Higher. Oh yeah, right there.

MELE: Oh baby, you taste so good.

PERSIS: Mmm yes lick it baby. Up and down. Oh. Whoa! Yes! Suck my pussy baby. Suck that pussy.

MELE: Puzzy. Yeah. I like it.

PERSIS: Yeah, you like that pussy?

MELE: Yeah! Love this puzzzyyy. mmm. [purrs like a cat]

PERSIS: Oh stop right there. No, don't stop! Just stop right there. Yes, lick that clit ... mmmm faster. Ah! Too fast! Slow down. Yes, yes, yes ohh yes just like that.

MELE: *(talks to Persis's pussy)* Hey, pussycat. You like that? Here. *(licks)* Oh, you hungry?

PERSIS: You talking to my pussy?

MELE: Yeah, and she's talking back. She said she wants to be fucked.

PERSIS: Mmm yes, she did say that...pussy whisperer.

MELE: How do you want me to fuck you?

PERSIS: Ask my pussy baby. Make me purr.

MELE: Shit. Alright, you asked for it.

PERSIS: HOLY FAAAAAATHER, ohhh!! Ohhhhhhhhh! WOW!

PERSIS breaks up with MELE

PERSIS: I've given this a lot of thought, Mele. I tried. I really tried, but I can't do it. I can't be with you. It has nothing to do with you. You're an amazing woman and you're perfect the way you are, but I'm seeing someone else. It is a man.

MELE: I hope you fucking get cancer of the twat.

PERSIS: Excuse me?

MELE: I said I hope you guys are really happy together like that.

PERSIS: Awwww, thanks, babe.

MELE and TINA (after breaking up with PERSIS).

MELE: Persis is in a relationship with a man.

TINA: What?! Girl, you don't deserve that. Forget her! Remember, *(sings chorus from Tina Turner's 'The best').*

MELE: Maybe it's time to go back to my roots.

TINA: Would you git some from a Samoan?

MELE: My mum said never to date any Samoans. I could be related to them.

TINA: Giiiiirl! They're long-distance relatives. It's all good. Besides, *(sings chorus from Tina Turner's 'What's love')*!

MELE: You're so fuckin' weird.

TINA: Get on Tinder, sister:

MELE: It's OkCupid if you want pussy.

TINA: Cast thy net wider thou fisher of lesbians.

MELE: What shall I call myself?

>   *TINA thinks, then gets on her phone.*

TINA: Creamy_Caramel.

MELE: Creamy_Caramel?

TINA: Mmmmm, yummy.

>   *MELE waits for responses ...*

TINDER #1

WHITE BULL DIKE: They call me Biscuit. You can take a bite outta me.

LOCAL BUTCHIE: SUP! I'm Paki. Like to cruise around? Maybe drink on the beach? I can play my gat while you dance.

FIRST TIMER: HI. I just got out of this long relationship with a man and I'm so over it. I've always been curious; I know I'm a lesbian. I kiss girls every time i'm drunk. Anyway, hope you can show me the ropes.

FAKE LESBO: Hiiii. Hoping you wanna have sum fun. I have a boyfriend, but he doesn't mind. I've been with girls before and i'm hoping to feel the touch of a woman again soon. Really soon. Really, really soon.

FIA[2] BLACK POLYNESIAN DYKE: Giiiiiiirl I jus wanna know: how you doin'? Hope you greedy as alllll hell cuz you gonna wanna experience whatever I can create, polish and manifest! My friends call me Slide and it would be a smooth and intense pleasure to slide inside.

HIPPIE WHITE LESBO: Kia ora. My name is Sandy. I love living on Waiheke. I love the beautiful beaches and taking long walks and watching the sun go down. Hope we can cradle each other's space sometime. Namaste.

Guitar.

SCHOLARLY POLYNESIAN LESBIAN (QUEEN KANUTRI): Hi Creamy_Caramel! Loved your profile. What do you think decolonizing love and the body means?

MELE: Hi Queen Kanutri … Wow, that's such a great question. Well, our views of love/body can be more gender-fluid for example or have more than one lover.

---

2 Wannabe.

MELE: A 'right lesbian'? I've had a lot of trouble with these terms when I was first coming out.

MELE: Wait. Let's meet…

TINA: Well, fisher of lesbians? What didst thou catcheth in the Lesbian Ocean?

MELE: A Queen …

MELE's first date with QUEEN KANUTRI

QUEEN KANUTRI: Why do you have a ukulele?

MELE: In case I get uncomfortable, I can just serenade you.

QUEEN K: You must be comfortable then.

MELE: For now. Until you start questioning me, then I just break out into song.

QUEEN K: Play something for me!

MELE: I'm not uncomfortable yet.

QUEEN K: Well then tell me about yourself. Why are you single?

MELE: I just haven't found the right one. Been hurt too many times now to want to start anything too serious with anyone.

QUEEN K: How have you been hurt?

MELE: What's your favorite song?

QUEEN K: OH NO! Answer the question!

MELE: I'll play you my favorite song.

QUEEN K: Nooo … tell me.

MELE: How bout you just sit there and I'll just sweep you off your feet with my terrible singing.

QUEEN K: Terrible? How are you supposed to sweep me off my feet if it's terrible?

MELE sings the chorus of Rhianna's 'Diamonds'.

QUEEN K: You're monogamous. I can tell.

MELE: What's wrong with that?

QUEEN K: Absolutely nothing. Except you're too sweet. I wouldn't want to hurt you. I'm anything but monogamous.

MELE: Yes! Monogamy. It's so ... Christian.

QUEEN K: It is!

MELE: I agree. And you're not.

QUEEN K: I'm not.

MELE: And as much as I'd like to pretend I'm not, I am.

QUEEN KANUTRI: You are.

MELE and TINA

TINA: So ... how was your date?

MELE: We had dinner. Walked on the beach. I brought my uke and serenaded her. It was very romantic. It was a romantic evening in Auckilagi between two 'queer' women. It was very precolonial romantic until we realised I was very ... postcolonial Christian.

TINA: Jesus Christ! did you get laid or what?

MELE: No.

TINA: Then guess it's back to the drawing board!

OKCUPID #2

'THE BETTE': I don't have tolerance for liars or bullshitters or people who are late. They waste my time and my time is the most precious thing I can give you, especially since I don't have much of it.

'THE MAX': Loyalty. I'm loyal and I expect my girl to be loyal. If a chick loves me, she should be by my side 24/7. That's what a partnership is. That's love. So if you were mine, I'd never leave your side, babe. Like never. Ever. Like seriously.

'THE JENNY': Is this ...Tinder? I'm sorry. I don't know what I'm doing here. I'm not ... I mean ... I ...

'THE MARINA': I love to travel. I love cozy sweaters and a good book. I have my own business and i'm always looking for new partnerships. What I'd really love is to get to know you. In the sack.

'THE SHANE': Whaddya say we just get outta here, get naked and fuck?

MELE turns Tinder off.

MELE and SHANE and GRANDMA LOLA

MELE: Oh shit! My gramma! Hi Grandma. This is my friend, Shane.

G LOLA: Shame?

MELE: Shane.

G LOLA. O ai Shame?

SHANE: Shane. It's nice to meet you.

G LOLA: Long time no see.

MELE: How are you?

G LOLA: With Jehovah's help, I'm okay. So how do you two know each other?

MELE: Oh, you know ...

G LOLA: Where are you from?

SHANE: East Coast.

G LOLA: Your friend is nice, but she looks like a man. Is she lesbian?

MELE: Grandma! It's none of our business!

G LOLA: You must know, if you're friends.

MELE: Sorry, Grandma, we need to get going.

G LOLA: So, Shane, what do you think about this gay marriage?

MELE: Grandma!

SHANE: I think everyone is entitled to the right to marry.

G LOLA: Are you aware what the Bible says?

SHANE Aue. We live in a different time. Maybe we can discuss it another time. Just you and me, okay?

MELE: Bye, Grandma.

Aunty Momi

Ahhh! Dat kurl is such a kood kurl. Very respectful ... It's ogay MELE don't haf a boyfren. But MELE is a gay. She cut her hair very short like a poi and she wea da poi clothes. Kalofae! But we still love MELE. MELE is so sweet, always take kea off eferyone, ah. Her dad my nephew. He was a kood man too befoa he left to be with those other womens. He used to always come by and bring ulu and taro fo me when he was a young poi. He and my huspand play cricket togetha. Ia. Puipui was a kood man. His daughter is jus like him, ah.

MELE, TINA and GINA (GINA)

TINA: Hi. Can I help you?

GINA: Hi. I'm Gina Davis.

TINA: Funny. I'm Tina Turner. Get it? Gina Davis. Tina Turner? *(Sings chorus from Tina Turner's 'The best'.)*

GINA: *(to MELE)* And you are?

MELE: Mele. Karamele. Like caramel, but Samoan.

GINA: Caramel … I like it.

MELE: I'd like to give you a personal tour around the offices.

GINA: Excuse me?

MELE: Just give me a minute and I'll be right out.

GINA exits.

TINA: I'm sorry! Caramel, but Samoan?! Buahahahaha!!!

MELE: I'd smear my caramel all over that.

TINA: You're disgusting.

MELE: Thank you. Now, if you don't mind, I'm going to give our new director a personal tour.

TINA: Whore.

MELE: Bye Ms. Turner!

MELE and TINA and MICHAEL

MELE: She's seeing someone else. I know it.

TINA: Did she say anything?

MELE: Yes, she said 'I forgot to change the sheets.' First thing she says as soon as she wakes up! No 'good morning,' 'hi,' 'how'd you sleep?' NONE OF THAT. 'I forgot to change the sheets'!

TINA: That does sound a bit strange to say first thing in the morning.

MELE: I was probably sleeping in someone else's fucking cum.

TINA: Excuse me I'm eating.

MELE: Ugh! I can't believe I fell for her.

TINA: She was probably just really wanting to change her sheets.

MELE: I'm gonna fuck someone. In her bed. A man!

TINA: Damn. That's. Dirty. Who's this man?

MELE: I don't know yet.

TINA: Tinder.

MELE goes on Tinder.

MICHAEL: Southside sole looking for his Polynesian princess. If this ad is up, so am I.

MELE: Lookin to keep you up all night.

MICHAEL: Hey.

MELE: Hey.

MICHAEL: Got a pic? Here's mine.

MELE: *(gasps)* Wow. Nice penis. Here's mine.

MICHAEL: Damn … you fine.

MELE: I'd like to run my fingers over that hard chest of yours.

MICHAEL: That's not the only thing that's hard.

MELE: Show me.

MICHAEL: I'll show you in person. Keen? What's your addy?

MELE: What's your name?

MICHAEL: I'm Michael. Yours?

MELE: Tina Turner.

MICHAEL and MELE fuck

MELE climaxes.

MELE: Mmm that felt so good. Thanks.

Michael: It's not over yet. I haven't cum.

MELE: Oh. Well … alright.

MELE looks bored and begins fake moaning.

Michael: Uce. Uce. Uce. I'm coming. Uccccccccce.

MELE feigns climax.

MICHAEL: That was mean. Can I use your shower?

GINA and MELE argue

MELE: What are you doing here?

GINA: I live here. Who the fuck was that?

MELE: Who?

GINA: Don't play me. That man that just left my apartment?

MELE: No one.

GINA: Did you just fuck a man in my bed? You did, didn't you?

MELE: Yeah. See how it feels?

GINA; What are you talking about?

MELE: I saw it. On your sheets. Somebody else's cum.

GINA laughs.

MELE: You're not even going to deny it, are you?

GINA: Come on. What makes you think you're worth being the only one? You're my bitch. I fuck you when I want, and I fuck somebody else when I want. You think you're special? You're not special. You wonder why you are the way you are? Lonely ... alone? Take a look at yourself Mele. You're pathetic.

MELE and BARMAN, drunk

INNER DEMONS whisper in the background as MELE is at the bar. They repeat their chant. Chant progresses getting louder.

INNER DEMON #1: Are you gay?

INNER DEMON #2: Are you straight?

INNER DEMON #3: What are you? Bi or bicurious?

INNER DEMON #1: Lesbian?

INNER DEMON #2: Queer?

INNER DEMON #3: Dyke?

INNER DEMON#1: Pretty boi?

INNER DEMON#2: Trans?

INNER DEMON #3: Pussy lover.

INNER DEMON #1: Pussy muncher.

INNER DEMON #2: Munch.

INNER DEMON #3: Munch her!

ALL: What are you?

MELE: Give me some JD.

MAN: You already came in once already.

MELE: I'm okay. Just give me the JD. Fuck ya then.

Lights change.

MELE: Jehovah, Yahweh, Great Spirit, Whoever you are, I'm begging you … *(Demon chant stops)* … please take my life or take this burden away from me. I can't help who I am, who you've created me to be. I can't go on living this lie. Take me or give me the strength to come out to my grandma. Please … help me. Please …

MELE post suicide attempt

MELE:
Fuck. I'm still here.
Fine.
Have it your way, Yahweh. Looks like we're coming clean.

MELE coming out to GRANDMA LOLA

G. LOLA: Oh Mele, it's so good to see you Long time I never see you.

MELE: Grandma, how you feeling?

G. LOLA: Oh, i'm good, with Jehovah's help. I can still go out in the ministry. I just use Bertha – that's what I call my walker.

MELE: How's your blood pressure?

G. LOLA: Oh, with Jehovah's help it's still good.

MELE: Look! I'm using the ring you gave me. I never take it off.

G. LOLA: Look so pretty on your finger. Maybe one day you can give it to your daughter.

MELE: I don't plan on having any kids.

G. LOLA: Oh, that's okay. You got time. Do you have a boyfriend yet?

MELE: Nope. No boyfriend.

G. LOLA: Would be good if you found you a nice boy in the congregation.

MELE: I'm not interested in men.

G. LOLA: What you mean?

MELE cries. GRANDMA wipes the tears away.

MELE: I'm … I'm gay.

GRANDMA recoils.

G. LOLA: A gay. But that's not right, Mele! That's not right in Jehovah's eyes. This is why you MUST COME BACK to the TRUTH, Mele! This is unnatural!

MELE: Gramma, This is just who I am. I can't change that! Jehovah made me this way.

G. LOLA: NOW YOU WATCH WHAT YOU SAY about Jehovah God!

MELE: I've always been afraid of killing you with my truth but … I can't lie anymore.

(Silence)

G. LOLA: A se lou valea. How you going kill me?

MELE: I dunno. Heart attack? Stroke? Aneurysm?

G. LOLA: I'm not dead. *(Pause)* But I am disappointed.

MELE: Grandma …

G. LOLA: Grandma is tired. Maybe you should go.

MELE: I love you Grandma.

GRANDMA LOLA doesn't say anything.

TINA tells MELE about The Back Room

TINA: They'll call you into a small room. There'll only be one window. You'll be able to see outside, but no one will be able to see you. There'll be three elders with their Bible and *Young People Ask* book. They'll open it up with a prayer and then tell you how someone saw you – you and your girlfriend kissing outside of Starbucks or something..

Then they'll tell you, *(as THE ELDER)* 'Mele, you know why we called you in here, don't you? You're a homosexual.' They'll ask, 'Who were you kissing outside of Starbucks? Did you have sex? What kind of sex did you have?'

'The Bible makes it clear that God designed sex to be engaged in only between a male and a female and only within the arrangement of marriage.'

'Now let's turn our bibles to Genesis, chapter 1, verse 27 and 28 – and when you're done with that, turn your bibles to Letivviticus 18:22 …

MELE: It's Leviticus.

TINA Whatever. 'Go on. Tell me what it says.'

MELE: I won't. I know what it says.

TINA: *(as herself)* That's the part when you're supposed to read the scripture.

MELE: I'm not reading it. I'm gonna tell them, 'I'm not reading it.'

TINA: Oh ... okay. Well this should be interesting. *(Goes into ELDER character)* 'You deliberately disobeyed me, Simba!' *(Laughs. After composing herself, continues)* Okay, seriously. 'Are you ready to sacrifice the hope of everlasting, your family and our worldwide brotherhood, so you can live as a homosexual?'

MELE: I do.

TINA: *(as herself)* Well then, you may kiss the bride.

MELE: It's too bad women can't be elders, Tina.

TINA: Mele, are you really gonna do it?

MELE: No sense convincing a rock to be a fish.

TINA: What does that even mean?

ELDER JOHN counsels MELE in The Back Room

ELDER: 'God loved the world so much he gave his only betgotten son.' That is an act of true alofa. Love. Despite people persecuting God's son, Jehovah and his son Christ Jesus chose to love the world unconditionally. Unconditionally.' Mele, you know why we called you into The Back Room, don't you? You're a homosexual. Dana from Congregation told us.

MELE: Whatta narc.

ELDER: 'The Bible makes it clear that God designed sex to be engaged in only between a male and a female and only within the arrangement of marriage.' Now read Genesis, chapter 1, verse 27 and 28 and, when you're done with that, turn to Leviticus 18:22. Go on.

MELE: I know what it says.

ELDER: What was that?

MELE: You're trying to change me but I'm not planning on changing.

ELDER: You understand the consequences?

MELE: I was avoiding this for years because I thought my grandma was gonna die of a heart attack once she found out I was gay and dis-fellowshipped but she isn't dead since, so …

ELDER: I'm disappointed in you. We'll be announcing it at the meeting this Sunday.

MELE: That's when I'll be doing your mum.

ELDER: What was that?!

MELE: I said I'll miss going doortodoor with your mum. Such a sweet lady.

TINA AND MELE ON TINDER #4

TINA: What's happening on OkCupid?

MELE: Not much.

TAMMY: I love crossfit & yoga, clubbing, fine wine and fine women. I love to sink my teeth into dark, curvy women with depth.
My ideal first date is dinner, walk on the beach …

MELE: CHEESY!

TJ: Hey I'm TJ. Just moved here from Matamata but i'm originally from down the line. I love hiking on my days off, so I could use a hiking buddy, eh?

FIRST DATE: Go on a hike, be spontaneous, end up lost some-where in the mountains, practicing yoga on a cliff.

MELE: E, ki`o. I'm gonna change my profile to 'Let's go get Ben and Jerry's and drink lots of wine.'

SUC: Hey ma. You're gorgeous.

MELE: Thank you.

SUC: I love yoga!

MELE: Next!

TINA: Damn you're a lesbian bitch. I dare you to make a date with the next girl that lesbians you. I mean, messages you.

MELE: Deal!

Swipes to next profile.

MELE: Oh. Queen Kanutri. It's you.

MELE: How's life?

QUEEN K: Busy.

MELE: If you transformed under a full moon, what would you be?

QUEEN K: A crocodile. I like to lay still while my prey swims above me. I have this fantasy where I'm a crocodile who catches all the fish I can. One day I catch a fish that's too big to swallow. The fish is made of gold and swims out from behind my sharp teeth, then turns into the most beautiful woman who I end up falling in love with. Let's meet again, Karamele.

MELE: Holy shit! Queen Kanutri wants to meet tonight!

TINA: You'll never get laid otherwise. I have the location. If anything happens, I'll know where to look for your body.

MELE: I'll be there at nine. Fluid: Bring any toys if you have any. I'll be waiting ...

Light change.

QUEEN K: Hi Mele. Aren't you happy to see me?

MELE: I ... I ... don't know.

QUEEN K: I've been thinking of you ever since our date. I feel like we didn't really give each other a chance. We just assumed that it wouldn't work and left it at that.

MELE: I ... I . .really REALLY want ... to experience you.

MELE: Crocodile?

QUEEN K: Be my fish?

They kiss.

Aunty MOMI

It's about damn time! Don't worry about them. You gotta take care of yourself. See? Feel good ah? You can't tell me it doesn't feel good. Not heavy no more. Now you watch. You gonna soar like a bird, I tell you. Nothing can stop you now except ya self. Now you got no more burden, you free to be whatevah you like and whoevah you are. You going surprise ya self, you watch. You thought you knew you, but now you really going get to know you. YOU! I tell you. Just like dat song? You know Dat song?! Da one! *(she sings)*: 'Shine bright like a diamond. Shine bright like a diamond.' Hahaha! Das you! Shine bright like a diamond, Mele! Shine bright.

Lights down on MELE and QUEEN KANUTRI.

`UA UMA/THE END

Isaako Si`uleo
Photograph: Courtesy of contributor

Isaako Si`uleo

My first memory is of my grandmother's face, my grandmother Laloifi. Yeah her face, I think, her voice. Her. She had that Ripley[1] face, saintly, eyes like moons, shining eyes, kind, that kind Ripley face. To me that's the prettiest. Her eyes always looked like they were smiling. Those were my earliest memories, her face, her voice, because I was really little when she died. I found her but I think it was too early, I was too young to ... I mean, I don't have any trauma about it. But it prepared me pretty well; I think I was three when she died; and then my grandmother Uagalu. And so many people died right after that.

Seems like people have been dying my whole life. So that was probably a good thing, in a way, for me. Most Americans never see dead people. They don't see people die; it's like something they don't want to think about. For me it's been so much of my life that I'm grateful it started really early, that it never really scared me, you know all that superstitious stuff.

I was happy as a child. My parents were Edward Milton McMullin and Tafaoga Amisone Mauga. Mauga, that's the clan name. I was the middle of three boys. My older brother got to get out, be a leader, and get in trouble, all that stuff. By watching him, when he got in trouble and stuff, it was really easy for me to watch him and be different, and to do what my parents wanted me to do, and that bought me my freedom really, as a kid, being able to please my parents, get good grades in school, do all the things they ask me to.

That word fa`afafine makes me think of my male aunties. I mean we called them uncles but they were always hanging out with the aunties, we thought of them as aunties; and they

---

1 Ripley – a totolua or mixed-blood family from `Upolu, Independent Sāmoa, and Leone Village, American Sāmoa.

acted like aunties, they talked like women. They were my mom's friends; Tilo and Fealo were their first names. They were always around; they were part of the church, the choir that my mom always sang in. They were always at ko`oga`i on Saturdays, at church events, and there were a lot of them.

Fealo, he wasn't big, just chubby, he dressed sharp, not flashy, just sharp, crisp, nice, same with Tilo, both of them. To me that was what fa`afafines were – are – guys that dress sharp and act like aunties. And my mom loved them; she loved them so much; that's all I needed to know. It was like when she was with her girlfriends – they played music, they'd sing and laugh and dance, have food. They were part of the church gang, my mom's church friends – the Samoan civic families, even when they went to other churches.

I've never felt different in terms of gayness. I mean I loved my mom, I loved her very much, but I just always wanted to be like my dad, that's what I've always tried to do. Sa`o is the word I'd use to describe him, upright, good, gentle, thoughtful and soft-spoken, humble and devoted; all the things that I admire, and courageous – he was my role model. Those are the values that I've always tried to live up to as much as I can. He was the best man that I saw as a child. When I became a man that's what I wanted to be.

I had a lot of conflicts but not around gender. I mean, I felt like a freak as long as I can remember, it wasn't because I was gay or whatever it was because I was different. I pretty much knew I was different in every way from every other kid I knew, in the things that I thought were interesting, and how I would pursue things, to the exclusion of other kids; I didn't play with other kids very much, I was by myself. I really enjoyed the company of some of them but every chance I got I was off by myself, reading, collecting bugs or rocks, some nerdy thing.

My parents always supported me in anything like that, if it was educational they said, 'Yes.' They would try to figure out a way to let me do, make it happen. I'm always grateful: by the time I was eighteen I had what I needed to survive in my unique path, which I believe my parents saw and prepared me for. They raised us each so differently.

I think I must have been fourteen, fifteen, and I fooled around with a cousin who was a couple years older. I fooled around a bunch of times. I loved it, it was great, and I still have warm memories of it, from about thirteen to seventeen. There was no gay world around me until about 1975–76, around there, then suddenly my whole neighborhood was gay. That was kind of shocking, it eventually drove me out of San Francisco – not just that, but largely that, it was kind of the last straw.

But up until I was eighteen I was in high school, it was my consuming interest, Lick-Wilmerding High School – they were two schools, one was a trade school, one was a college prep school, and they merged. When I graduated our units were exactly twice as many as any other California high school. Someone had just created this minority scholarship; two black guys and me, we were the first. It was a total culture shock in a way, it was all boys, all the rich boys who couldn't cut it in the fancy private schools; they were the outsiders of the money class. I'd say it was two-thirds Jewish. By the time I got out of high school I was quite familiar with all the holy days and festivals, I'm really grateful, got exposed to locks and bagels and cream cheese and chopped chicken liver, all the stuff I really love to this day. I'm starting to realise that everything just changes all the time, even our perception of things. And I was just a kid, not just a kid – a freak, a big nerd, loved school and just kept myself busy and was very happy.

I don't think there were any professionals in the Islander community in those days, among the Samoans, Hawaiians, Tongans, Fijians who were around. And there was probably only one store that sold kalo and coconuts and stuff. Tauoa's church was the first I remember. I still miss things about it. The singing. It's so beautiful to me that it's hard for me to describe. It's a kind of harmony that I think can only come from people who think communally.

Everybody at school was completely different from my family

and me. I liked some of the kids fine, I wasn't anti-social … it was San Francisco in the sixties, my friends were Pedro Rodriguez, and Cathy Wong, and Michael Novak, and Marto MacDowell. It was like a movie, all my classes in school, and I realised we were one of the few schools in the country at the time where it was desegregated and apparently perfectly normal. Nobody seemed to be tripping about it at all, except I started seeing it on TV in other parts of the country – but for us it was already normal, and there they couldn't even stand the thought of it.

San Francisco was a lot smaller then than it is now, but what's important about that city is that it hasn't really changed, there's a spirit about this city that attracts like spirits from other places. And I think it has become a part of the culture about the city; and even in California we were different from L.A. and Sacramento, other places. It was always an adventurous progressive-minded place, attracted those kinds of people.

And when Islanders came here it was a fertile ground for them, because most of the country would have been so hostile. I think the community took root incredibly fast. That was the one feature of my childhood that was constant – that there was always people coming from the islands, there were waves of people through the sixties. It almost seemed like people had to bring people – I don't think suddenly people could just start coming, people were always bringing people, it grew exponentially that way, in a sense of community. You had shared language, culture, religion, and a lot of shared things. You were in a foreign environment; it made you cling closer to the people that are familiar to you. I think there's a certain kind of community that only exists in that window of time, in that first window of immigration. I think all immigrants must experience that wherever they come from.

My mom, I loved her so much, her steadiness, she was always right about certain things. I never in my life felt I was not loved or wanted, I never felt that way; I always felt loved and wanted and appreciated. They were tough, demanding, very strict discipline, but I never really suffered, I never got in trouble, because all the things they wanted to do I liked doing, to please them. Even after they've gone, I still feel the same way; I still want to please them; that's part of whom I am.

Mom when she was with Dad she was like a girl, her voice was girly, the way she talked to him was different from the way she talked to everyone else in the world, her voice was soft. She was incredibly strong, determined, uncompromising in her ideas, but generous and loving, and when she was with him that was all you saw. The way he was with her, it was the only time he was almost goofy-looking to me. Most of the time he was always incredibly cool and smart, everything I always wanted to be. But with her he was like a boy, a boy and a girl in love.

The fire. The fire was at All Hallows Parish in Bay Short, Hunters Point area; their hall was really big. They were at the time raising money to build a Samoan Congregationalist church, the Samoan Civic Association. Everything was growing fast; people were scrambling to make a connection, for their kids, networking. It was May 23rd, 1963. I remember everyone going off; they were all excited about it, girls making clothes. Everyone gathered at our house, went off in a caravan.

I guess at the time there weren't the fire codes to require the exits to be opened, unlocked, so the doors were chained, chained shut. The place caught fire. What I heard was that it was an accident involving the fire dance, that someone had tin kerosene that got knocked over. The flames spread too fast for anyone to do anything. And people panicked, and started stampeding out. And really not that many got out before they were falling on top of each other so that no one was getting out. That's why so many people died.

My dad at the time was outside smoking a cigarette and saw the first people running out, and he ran in to find my mom and he actually got her just as people were starting to fall. Some people were just making it out but right behind them everyone was starting to fall because they were pressing so hard from behind. My dad pushed my mom out but she fell in the doorway so she was burned in the back of her legs; where he fell he got burned all the way up. He was just inside and she was just outside the door.

I think it was the biggest percentage of Polynesian people who died that night. I know the funerals went on for weeks. And for the next year or two, every Samoan was in the hospital all the time, in the waiting rooms. That fire changed the fire codes about exits. It also changed the hospital policies about visitors: they let one or two visitors at a time; suddenly all the waiting rooms were full of Samoans – fifteen, twenty people there and their kids, they'd be singing for hours. They'd never seen that before, they didn't know how to deal with it. But I don't think anyone was keen to discourage it, it was clearly an important part of our culture. When someone was suffering people shared their burden, they'd sing. It was like, which hospital were you going to today; people went together to make it easier to sing together, hymns mostly.

There were ko`oga`is every Saturday, I'd get to see all my cousins, they brought guitars, ukulele, beer and food, all their kids, and we'd play all day. By evening they were playing music and singing. My mom was in a few months before she was well enough to come home. My dad was in for a few years before he could come home. I don't think he ever really recovered; he had burns in some of his internal organs. He was able to go back to work a few times for short periods. He had lost all his hair, was terribly scarred. He had been strong before but was never again.

He used to pile us in the car, drive somewhere, go swimming, up until the fire it was always busy, busy, busy … The next day after the fire was my birthday, but since then, birthdays were whatever; just please don't have anyone die. It was amazing, the few people who had not gone to the luau got together, and immediately sorted out who was taking care of the kids. They figured out my Uncle Sam and Aunty Lupe in the south in Monterey would come and get us for the summer – they just came and got us.

San Francisco in the sixties, the world was an exciting place. There were so many places that were free, libraries, museums, available to a kid like me who went to public school and had no money, rode the bus. I got to see so much; I was aware of all these things going on in the world.

I became aware of the war in Vietnam pretty early because my one uncle had died early in the war, in the early sixties, it was part of my consciousness and to know how he died – it always affected me. He was Uiga Amisone, my mom's brother. I just remembered that war was terrible, it caused my family a lot of sadness. As the sixties unfolded I felt more and more that way. It wasn't just my family that was suffering, it affected the way I see the world. I think in general Samoans are great soldiers, I have family in the military, and they make excellent soldiers, they know how to put 'we' ahead of 'self', which is difficult for Americans. I always feel off the scale, the left and right to me are equally offensive. When I was in my twenties trying to figure out the world, that's when Harvey Milk got killed, Patty Hearst, all that shit was going on … Being from San Francisco, it fueled my passion for politics.

The bar I worked at, at Church and Sanchez, turned gay; it was called the Mine Shaft, it went from having a gay night to primarily a gay clientele in '75. It wasn't just the bar the neighborhood changed. That's when I was first aware. Before '75 you really didn't notice as much, then thousands and thousands flooded the city, that changed things so fast. For me I felt like they were invaders, they were unwelcome, I didn't understand what their mission was. It didn't matter to me – gay people, to me, I didn't feel anything in common with them. It's not like I was anti-gay – my roommates were gay too.

Ninety-nine-point-nine percent of all these new guys who showed up in the middle of the seventies were just bourgeois middle class, all they wanted to be was party boys, they had this whole weird fantasy trip they turned into a culture. It's part of why I left. More than ninety percent of the guys that were coming were white, of course, they were there to do drugs, life was a big sex party, and it really made the neighborhood unpleasant. So … hell no …

I liked the world that they displaced – we called it the Bible

Belt because there were all these churches, so many; and on Sunday mornings, when everyone was so hungover, you couldn't sleep because there were so many church bells. And then you'd hear the music, organ music and people singing. Of course all the bar people kept complaining but I was happy to get up, do my laundry, I liked it, even though I didn't belong; I liked it better than sex clubs, foufou middle-class fashion crap.

Have I ever done drag? Once my friends did me up in '75 as Donna Summer in the Castro, with a bottle of whiskey in my hand. People on the street were singing her song as I walked by. I was miserable, I didn't care, I was this big ugly Donna Summer, people were saying 'Hi,' I was like, 'Fuck off,' and I didn't care. At the party flat I propped myself against the wall with my bottle of whiskey, my friends kept checking me as I slid down the wall slowly, until I was on the floor with an empty bottle.

I've been a carpenter all my life. The most important thing for me is, I realised, I tend to be kind of cerebral and it made me balanced; and since I didn't have anything else on my horizon, I decided it would be good for me. I like doing physical work, I like the way it makes me feel, healthy and strong, being a plus in the world instead of a minus. It's honest work, and there were not that many opportunities when I got out of high school. Most guys were getting drafted, or running away to Canada, or doing drugs – that was everything around me.

When I was living in the communes I got involved in the anti-war movement, also with this one group of people who I later found out were terrible criminals. It got pretty bad – I had to change my name and move out of the city. I found out two of the kids that worked for them died. Haight Street was a big mess. I had to run hard.

I couldn't sleep, but when I finally did fall asleep my grandmother Laloifi came to me the way I remembered her, same face, but I don't think she was old. She told me several things, but the important thing is she gave me the name I needed: Siuleo, means echo, simultaneous vibrations, in the water, waves patterns cross patterns.

When my father was dying my brothers came and found me. We didn't talk much, my dad and I, I just held his hand, and this was '79. When he died I packed up and moved to Portland Oregon, didn't talk to my family for fifteen years. I was terrified of these criminal people I was involved with finding me. I just disappeared, because when my brothers found me I felt these other guys could find me.

I had a big glassed in apartment where I could watch Mt Saint Helens blow up for a couple years, I watched it blow up, it looked like a mountain with half of it blown off, giant steam clouds drift for miles and miles, you always knew which way the wind was blowing. It was Pele. I felt it was the sign of a good move. Then I moved to Seattle doing construction work, or bartending. Through the Eighties I was back and forth between Seattle and New York. I got really strong at thirty: I put on fifty pounds of muscle doing construction; I could turn my brain off. I worked for myself a lot as a contractor, sometimes for giant highways.

In retrospect I realised my first friend that I lost to AIDS – she and I escaped the communes together – she and I were like brother and sister; she was half Mexican, half Japanese, one of the most beautiful women I'd ever seen in my life, porcelain skin, Aztec nose, black blue hair, Sandra. Commune life was so boring, these hippies were annoying, all these white kids dabbling in Hinduism and art and politics, blah, blah, blah, debate about bullshit.

Sandra and I couldn't wait to get out of there. We lived in the Castro; I squatted with some guys in a place on Fillmore. She met a guy named Steve, I was happy for them. I was in New York about '84 or '85; another friend came to visit and said Sandra had died … It was real mysterious, she was sick, kept getting sicker and was gone. Steve went into a Buddhist monastery in Berkeley. It was a few years after that I began losing all my friends and thought back, that Sandra was the first one.

About '85 people were pretty freaked out. In New York they were dropping like flies – which totally shocked me, you didn't hear any about it anywhere else in the country. By the time

I got back to Seattle, a couple years later, people were dying there too.

It was around '85 the first AIDS quilt was laid out in Washington DC, we were there when they brought out the quilt for the first time, they kept bringing it out, bringing it out on the Washington Mall – that big place – and, like that, it was so clear how many people were dying. There was a square for each person, and the president still hadn't said the word AIDS on TV. They were all terrified. They couldn't control it.

That was '85 and I think Sandra died in '83. I lost friends. I lost all my friends. My partner Charlie and me, there's almost no one left whom we knew from before. They were just pretty much all gone, just Charlie left and me.

I met Charlie in New York: friends dragged me out, said we have a friend we'd like you to meet, he's really boring like you, a big nerd ... They were right. We went over to his apartment, which was on East 6th Street in the Village, tiny wretched place but it did have a fireplace, it was very charming.

The first thing I saw was a stack of Polaroid photographs, and I was the only person I knew of who had a 1950s camera like that, it weighed a ton but took beautiful pictures, and Charlie had the same one. There was a stack of *Chick* publications made to scare people about Hell, gay people, drinkers, whatever the hate of the day, the most vicious and frightening ones I'd seen, so much so I collected them – and Charlie had the same ones. It was too uncanny, I almost thought my friends had set me up, were clowning me. But he was like that. I thought, Okay he has my attention now.

We started hanging out immediately. And I love Charlie very much. I'm so grateful to have spent twenty-five years of my life with him. We didn't make any provisions at all to live this long. I turned positive just before New Years in '98. Charlie was positive the first time we got tested in '90. We were the last ones of my friends to get sick, so by then we were already in full care and burial mode. That's all we had been doing for several years, changing sheets. We all die, I'm just glad I knew them. By '89 we'd prepared ourselves to die, it just didn't seem possible we were going to live much longer.

Somehow when Charlie got his diagnosis something snapped in us. We saw something on telephone poles called People Curing AIDS Network. I felt akin to them, they were only half a dozen, sometimes ten, these guys trying experimental treatments, alternative therapies. There were drugs, but you just died. But they were like us; they weren't going to die.

It kept us going, it changed the way we thought: I'm not going down without a fight, and I'm not sitting here to die. The main guy was Randall from Texas, always a new boyfriend in tow, very compelling, honest. The other was a Kiwi named Greg, looked like Wallace in Wallace and Gromit.

We started doing ozone injection therapy, juicing, every kind of tea, for months before AZT came out. Suddenly there were therapies and Charlie started doing AZT. It was a while before they started having antiretrovirals.

We moved to Seattle. I was a cable tech, loved being up high; I have boxes of photos I took up on the pole. And then I came home again and had years of time to enjoy with Mom, there was a lot of catching up to do.

Memories of the time before the fire, they were all so beautiful.

Roger Stanley
Photographer: Evotia Tamua

Tootooali`i Roger Stanley

I'm Tootooali`i Roger Stanley. I was born and raised here in Apia, so I've been a town girl all my life!

I've been born into an afakasi family and I'm the second to the youngest of eight siblings, my dad passed away when I was twelve. I have been a fa`afafine all my life since I come to senses in life growing up in the town area and I happened to have these strange feelings that I was attracted to men. I loved to do girls' stuff like picking up the rubbish, sweeping the house, helping my family at a very young age.

Because I grew up in my nuclear family and being brought up in town I reckon it was easier for me compared to other fa`afafine brought up in the rural areas, so I reckon there is a big difference simply because where they were raised regarding the acceptance of fa`afafine. For me I was free I didn't get punished for being fa`afafine. Growing up I saw a lot of fa`afafine in my area and my parents had a lot of fa`afafine friends so there wasn't any problem growing up as a fa`afafine, there wasn't any time where my parents were trying to stop or limit my freedom to express myself as a fa`afafine.

I did a lot of schooling in Sāmoa and I was lucky because it was a mixed school and I got to hang out with the girls and there were a lot of fa`afafine in school. Going to college was challenging for me because I had to cut my hair short, no makeup and you had to wear a male uniform, but it was all right, I survived and I have no bad emotion or setbacks, nothing to worry about.

I'm brought up in a Christian family. I often got told off by my mum for not getting up on Sunday morning to attend the church service and obligations like White Sunday; my mum wanted me to attend two church services in a day and that was too much for me. I used to be active in drama and skits in church. I still go to church on Sundays; it's just normal now.

It was my luck to get a career in public service because I was a bit naughty when I was in college for not studying hard and I was really into the world of fa`afafine. I was constantly persuaded by other fa`afafines to get dressed up and hang out in nightclubs having fun and experience having sex with guys and older men; however all that affected my education at the college level. I have to admit I wasn't performing as well as I thought.

But I was the lucky one that made it through finishing bursary and university, and never in my wildest dreams that I would end up at university, but university was the worst! I was outing every night enjoying my alcohol and enjoying dancing and enjoying having sex with men who came along my way ... but I always kept in mind that I knew I had a purpose which was to complete my education and must go back to Sāmoa and serve my family.

When I went to Fiji for schooling it was a culture shock as, although Fiji is a Pacific island there were a lot of differences in terms of development compared to Sāmoa, and I reckon Fiji is more advanced than Sāmoa. I got to meet all sorts of people from the Pacific region, it's a melting pot of cultures and I felt like I fit in well in this multiethnic and multiracial community. I introduced the world of fa`afafine culture into Suva in the mid nineties and it came at a time where Fiji was less tolerant against fa`afafine, so I was able to give back confidence and open the door for Fijian fa`afafine.

When I go back to Fiji now I see Fijian fa`afafine fully dressed in women's clothes and in makeup and I'm glad I was able to inspire them. For fa`afafine dressing up as a woman in Fiji is considered a fraud and most were declined entrance at the nightclubs. But every time I go out I was the only one that was allowed in the nightclubs because I befriended the bouncers and security where I used my personality and my character to get my way into the club.

One of the things I have to say about Sāmoa is that Samoan parents have so much expectation of their children who travel overseas for education. There a lot of competition here and knowing the villages, the mothers and the fathers love to praise their children publicly and it comes with pride. But when you come back failed, that's considered a big disgrace to your family. So here I was doing my clubbing and alcohol but keep telling myself I had to complete my education so I can get a proper employment. So when I came back I was doing economics and management but my dad really wanted me to do law, but because of my life and the way I went through during high school I just couldn't do law.

So I came back looking for a job in government and one of the first jobs I did was community work, and from there I became a policy analyst for public services commission – so my interest in policy work began from there. Now I have reached just over ten years in public service and working as a senior policy analyst in social services for the Ministry of Women's Affairs in Sāmoa.

One of my reasons to develop the Sāmoa Fa`afafine Association first begun back in the days when I was a real showgirl in high school and clubbing with many young fa`afafine friends and just took it to the streets and you name it, we did it. So my passion began from there and when we were on the streets doing prostitution and what not and we got to experience some of the worst incidents in life and we were very unsafe on the street, and most of the things we did were very unsafe. So I got exposed to it at a very early age to the world of fa`afafine.

From there I gathered all my knowledge and understanding of what should be the ideal way for fa`afafine to move across, and it was from university I was empowered through education that challenged my own twisted thinking ... And I know fa`afafine are all not just good for having sex or for little bit of money or cabaret entertainment; I knew we can do much more than that.

I got invited to join the alumni of the ex-students of the University of the South Pacific and Sāmoa College. But when I went along to both functions I began to see that men dominated these gatherings and women, and then I thought: why not set up something for fa`afafine alone? Because I knew that issues affecting fa`afafine wouldn't be a priority of theirs. So I stopped going to the alumni gatherings where there were only three or four fa`afafine in attendance and we were a minority.

Being a fa`afafine myself I always enjoy sitting in fa`afafine gatherings, it's always good fun over a bottle of vodka or whatever. In Sāmoa there are already men's association and women's association established, so why not a fa`afafine association? And besides, the fa`afafine community has raised a lot of money for charity over the years yet they are never recognised for it – so it's also to create awareness of our contribution to the wider community. The Sāmoa Fa`afafine Association really is to meet the needs and the welfare for fa`afafine to gain fair employment, and to assist in health, social issues and monitor the human rights of fa`afafine.

The idea of having the current Sāmoa Prime Minister Tuilaepa Aiono Sailele Malielegaoi as our lead patron of the Sāmoa Fa`afafine Association was an idea of mine when I was working at the prime minister's office. It was when we were just about to launch the Sāmoa Fa`afafine Association and we first thought we should have a female minister, but they were already patrons of other association.

So after getting the running around I walked straight into the prime minister's office with a one-page letter inviting him to be the patron of the association and launch the association and to meet all these obligations. The prime minister then read the letter and ticked everything in the letter. People say, 'What were you thinking?' Well if he is the prime minister and the father of the nation and we were at early stages of forming our association, so why not get the toppest of them all to support us? And the prime minister has been a big help for us and he was a big boost to the association. And he's been the patron of the Sāmoa Fa`afafine Association since we first launched our association in 2006. When he became a patron it was the talk of the nation but in a good way.

I also opened the door in the public service of Sāmoa, being the first Samoan fa`afafine to come to work fully dressed in my puletasi and wearing lipstick. But I think also I managed to be at the right time at the right place because I entered the public service when it was at the peak of the Sāmoa public services reform. And the one of the main principles of the reform was avoiding discrimination in matching up with the international standard. It was so spot-on with my arrival, which protected my identity as a fa`afafine in the public service. So I just dressed up and did my own thing at work.

In the 1980s and '90s I never saw many fa`afafine who were dressed and living as women; instead I saw fa`afafine who wear men's clothes in public gatherings. But I began meeting up with other fa`afafine who came back to Sāmoa after graduating from university and they were fa`afafine who appeared publicly as women, which was fairly new to me. I still remember my boss at the time was a woman and she didn't care what I looked like or for my dress code as long as I performed well and do what is expected of me in my job description and to serve the public service. So after ten years in the public service I've been promoted as a senior policy analyst.

But I have to say I now see many fa`afafine graduating university, which is good, and they are now starting to wear their puletasi, growing their hair and wearing earrings and lipstick, which is good – but for me I'm not too keen on that stuff as long as they look professional and performing well in the workforce. Because a formal employment is not a place where you have a vacation or have a picnic because at the end of the day you have to go back home, and still serve your country and your family through your work to get some money for your bread and butter. But of course for your siblings and your parents waiting at home and also the church, oh, get scolded by my mum every single Sunday for not going to church!

The review of the Crime Ordinance Act came at a very good timing for Sāmoa and for us fa`afafine because the government of Sāmoa has decided to have the current laws to be reviewed simply because the law of the nation has been adopted from New Zealand in 1961 since our Independence. So there are legislations that are irrelevant to Sāmoa and there is also the prosecution for public female impersonation that has never been enforced which really refers to us fa'afafine but it has never been enforced by the law enforcement.

I'm really glad we are taking steps in dealing with these matters because the Human Rights Council around the world has pressured the Government of Sāmoa and Sāmoa is trying to catch up with the rest of the world in moving forward. So I reckon that's why Sāmoa created the Sāmoa Law Reform Commission where we the Sāmoa Fa'afafine Association were invited to submit anything in the current laws that we thought that affect us fa'afafine one way or the other.

I was very strong in gathering my girls and my executives and of course with the assistance of our qualified fa'afafine lawyers. And I'm so happy that this work was not done by men lawyers and the woman lawyers but by our own fa'afafine lawyers. I'm so glad that I was heading it while I was the president of the association at the time where I did all the yelling and the coordination. Because I'm not a lawyer and I don't have the legal background but I was at the forefront of just making it happen! So we can make the submission for a reform of a law that criminalises fa'afafine, for the Sāmoa Law Reform Commission. According to the CEO of the commission the cabinet has already endorsed it, so it's being discussed in Parliament.

My advice for young fa'afafine, without sounding like a contestant from Miss World, is that education is the key to success – and it's never gone wrong with me, especially with my personal experience. During high school I was all over the place, like clubbing, socialising, alcohol and never-ending boys, and I got to the stage where I didn't want to join a group for cabaret shows. I'm glad my mum was strong in keeping me focused. So my best advice for fa'afafine is to get good education.

Employment is here in Sāmoa for all you can grab; we have never faced an incident where fa'afafine been discriminated for employment, and you can always apply and get accepted. Sāmoa is going to build a Human Rights Commission here soon and people are going to be very careful with all their actions against fa`afafine or whoever.

I also wish to keep playing a good role model for young fa`afafine who are struggling to find their place. Always be good to your family because your family will take care of you at the end. That's what makes us unique from all other fa`afafine in the world; because other fa`afafine in the world, they are neglected from their families and by everyone because they never love their families and helping their families with whatever that's needed.

So if you're with your family then no one can take away your fa`amanuiaga [blessings] and everything.

Stephen Stehlin
Photographer: Evotia Tamua

Taualeo`o Stephen Stehlin

My Samoan chiefly title is Taualeo`o from the village of Sagone, which is my grandmother's village in Savai`i. My first name is Stephen and my second name is John after my father and my last name is Stehlin, it's Swiss; it's not German it's Swiss.

My great-great-grandfather came to Sāmoa about 1870 or so and settled in Savai`i so my great-grandfather was born there, my grandfather was born there and my father was born in Sāmoa. And I was born here in New Zealand. My mother is palagi so I guess I'm a bit of a mixture and I was always taught to be proud of my Samoan roots and that's how I identify myself.

I grew up in Manurewa with a palagi mum and a Samoan dad. In those days it was working class and aspiring. There was only one other Samoan family at my school and they too were afakasi – with a palagi dad. So I guess we were always different. I remember my parents sitting me down as a child to teach me about the 'color bar'. Certainly we were not palagi and there were so few Samoan families that there was no real Samoan community – just families. My grandfather and aunt and uncles arrived later. We would spend Sundays with them. I felt envious of my cousins from Sāmoa as they could speak Samoan. My grandmother spoke little English but my grandfather was a great orator in both languages. They were very religious.

Growing up as a child I always had a problem with 'belonging' – I never quite knew where I belonged and I had to learn that. I grew up in a very palagi environment because that's what New Zealand was like in the 1950s. I was born in 1957, so that was the basis of it. The first point of difference is that I am not the same as everybody else: we were not Anglo-Saxons and we were brown. So that colored my thinking. I was quite isolated. I had seen fa`afafine and they were always negative stereotypes – well, that was my impression. But I never knew anyone properly. Certainly I did not know anyone my own age.

As I grew older my grandmother would say she would take me to Sāmoa to get a girlfriend. In my closeted mind I thought a boyfriend would be more like it. So neither Samoan and not white either. People say, 'Oh you're a Kiwi, you don't look like a Samoan.' Well, that's their perception. You react according to how other people perceive you and people perceive me in 1960s growing up in New Zealand. I was certainly not a palagi. So I chose to be Samoan.

Then as my sexuality became apparent, I came to understand it because I resisted it for quite a while. It was a gradual realisation with me – that I was unlike other guys. I had no end of opportunities with girls but it would have been late teens that I realised that I was gay but hoped it wasn't true! I had had gay experiences early in my teens and lots of nothing but Catholic guilt! I needed to belong to something as well, so I came out later in life. When I did it around the time of the Homosexual Law Reform,[1] I guess that gave me some sense of belonging to a tribe.

So by my twenties I knew that I was gay but devoted myself to looking after my family. But I grew unhappy in my closet. I had brief hurried and unspectacular liaisons. One of the first things I did was to call a helpline. It took me days to summon up enough courage just to do that. The guy on the other end was so sweet. From there I went to the occasional meeting – it all seems so quaint now. I did this for quite a while and lived a curious double life. I worked in the Telephone arm of the New Zealand Post Office, where we would connect long distance calls – the Toll Exchange. The Tolls was a very disparate group of characters, which was full of gay people and a lot of fun.

Gradually I reached a point when I could not 'confirm or deny' any longer. It began quietly when someone at work asked me if I was gay and I surprised myself when I simply said yes. Then I began to tell friends, beginning with people whose friendship I

---

1   New Zealand's Homosexual Law Reform Act of 1986.

could afford to lose. My family was the last point. After a period of depression my father guessed it. Little was said but he did say that he had suspected it for a while and that I was still his son and that my happiness was all that mattered. My mother was concerned that I did not get AIDS. So my coming out was like others', in that it is a long process.

So Sāmoa first and being a gay man and then I put the two of them together. I belong to this other group called fa`afafine, so I'm very happy and content and I'm thrilled to see the support networks and the development of fa`afafine as a valued group within Samoan culture and within New Zealand culture as well.

I was thirty when I joined TVNZ[2] after many years of fruitless application. In those days many started their careers as television assistants. Pacific people were virtually nonexistent at TVNZ but there was *Tagata Pasifika*,[3] which was very young and very underresourced. Only two Pacific people worked on the show in those days. I started working on a Māori magazine called *Koha*,[4] and I worked on lots of other shows, but had my eye on TP, while applying for any job I could.

I was there for a while, and as Tagata Pasifika was in the same department where I was, I quickly became friends with Susana and Iulia. I eventually got a production manager job there, which taught me about budgets and managing people and resources. I bounced around and became producer in 1992.

Tagata Pasifika helped me be attuned to minorities because, not only we are minorities within minorities, but we were also making a show for Pacific people around a time where there was gross racism and gross misunderstanding. Fortunately the show is still going. It has become an institution now – next year it turns thirty. From its earliest beginnings it has strived to be the

2 Television New Zealand – nationally owned, commercially funded broadcaster for New Zealand and parts of the Pacific Islands region.

3 The main New Zealand television news and interview show for and by Pacific Island peoples, begun in 1987.

4 The first New Zealand Maori television show for and by Māori, begun in 1980.

Pacific voice – Pacific people telling Pacific stories. And so it has changed as the audience has changed. The biggest change is now upon us as we straddle the traditional television world and the brave new global digital world.

In the thirty years we've seen the mainstreaming of Pasifika culture and it is the cultural definition of this country; it is fantastic. I'm so proud of it. When you see that people are beginning to understand, you know, where would the All Blacks be without us? So we got the sporting prowess, we just got to lift our educational achievement and build on our artistic success, from my point of view. I can see two running in parallel, you know, it's given the country a definition and a point of difference. We compare that to Australia and people say we are alike? We couldn't be more different.

I think the representation of fa`afafine has gone from objects of derision and to where I say we're valued members of society. If we look at the work of pioneers like Fuimaono Karl Pulotu-Endemann at the time of Homosexual Law Reform, and at the time of the AIDS epidemic – I mean, we still have an AIDS epidemic, but when that was challenging everything around the status quo, it had challenged the Pacific community as well. I salute the courage and leadership of the Pacific people involved with the Pacific Aids Trust, like Karl, and Louisa Crawley, Ete Laufiso and Molly Fiso. These people were able to change community attitudes.

I recall covering condom use at church meetings – something that would have been unheard of in the past. Goodness me, that is a huge change for the Pacific communities and for the Samoan community to do. But we had to do it. I'm not saying that we are there: we still have problems in that regard and we have problems with acceptance. But for the Pacific communities, the epidemic meant that we had to face up to some realities and that involved talking about sex and rather than using fa`afafine as negative stereotypes we had to turn that around and embrace it. This was difficult for highly religious communities like the Pacific ones – and the struggle continues.

During my personal life, I found a boyfriend and learnt about relationships. Being gay became cool, although I am still guarded with people I do not know – but I am more at peace with myself as I broach sixty. When TVNZ outsourced *Tagata Pasifika* in 2014, I was recovering from some major surgery. I am focused on getting my health to a better level. With my colleagues, Ngaire Fuata and John Utanga, we formed a company (SunPix Ltd) and bid for the show. The company is now in its second year. Ngaire and John are the producers and I am the old guy in the corner signing off invoices and doing health and safety.

The development for fa'afafine over time has gone from where they were objects of derision – and we still have that comedy aspect of it – but it's people like Yuki Kihara that has taken a political stance in their art and Fuimaono Karl Pulotu-Endemann and his work in the health arena, where we can say, 'We are valued members of this society and we have something to contribute here and you can take us seriously,' because we are also knowledge keepers as well.

For young fa'afafine I'm sure that they all already do gravitate towards one another and find friends ... when you're alone, you cannot do anything in this world alone, you got to belong. If I can say to young fa' fafine, you belong to a huge group of very smart people that will support you. Just make yourself known and no one will judge you and everyone will support you. But you got to be part of the team, you got to be part of the tribe. And it is our tribe: be proud of it. Fa'afafine already have a place – not as entertainers but as the smart, intelligent people they are. I am full of pride when I see people like Yuki and Phylesha[5] take on the world stage.

The question around the future of Pacific television is more adequately answered by what is the future of free-to-air television – it's online, of course; but how we generate an audience of some critical mass remains to be seen. At the moment, as unsatisfactory as a morning television slot is, it still

---

5   Phylesha Brown-Acton – transgender activist with Pasifika LGBTQI.

has a huge following ... But the kids are not watching television the way we used to.

Fa`afafine find a place in the world of art, intellectualism, academia, and as cultural guardians – the ones who know the family histories, the protocols and the connections in our small world.

Alex Su`a

I'm a lawyer by profession. I live in Sāmoa; I'm staying with my parents in Vaivase Uta in `Upolu Island, Sāmoa. My mom is from Moata`a, and my father is from Samusu Aleipata. I'm here at the Outgames Human Rights Conference held in Wellington because a group of us, including myself, have been offered scholarships as delegates from Sāmoa. I'm a human rights activist as far as it relates to lesbian, gay, bisexual, transgender and intersex people, including fa`afafine.

I grew up knowing that I'm fa`afafine. According to my very clear recollection, I don't think I was 'made' into a fa`afafine. I knew this when I was very young, because I was the fourth child from the eldest, two boys, then a girl, then me, then my twin sisters, and then the youngest sister, and the youngest one is my brother.

So growing up after a sister I always had preference of dresses. And I remember White Sundays when children are often given the best dress, new things ... And I always remember I had that urge for my sister's dress, and the hair ribbons. I remember I was very young and I had those urges. Also when my sister had her birthdays and stuff, I always remember asking my mom, 'Can I have that doll? Can I have the cooking utensils?' The toys, I always liked girls' stuff, when I was young. I had always been with my female cousins.

I know my mother's father was very strict. I always remember and know that I was acting very normal, I was always normal, doing things normal, but there were times he would say, 'Why are your feet just like this? Why are you talking like that? Why are you walking like that?'

So, every day after school, I would always have that hesitance, feeling of fear, of going back to my grandparents' place. Because

Alex Su`a
Photographer: Evotia Tamua

usually my grandfather would ask me, 'Now this is when you have to walk like a boy.'

Then I would have to practice myself, walking like a boy; my uncles, cousins, would be laughing at me while I'm doing my parade. I remember there was one time, I wished I could just get what they were expecting of me. You know, I tried to walk like one, but I couldn't.

'No, no, no, no, no! Koe fa`asa`o lau savali pe ka le guku, a!?'[1]

And then I'd always wonder, 'What's wrong with me?' So I tried to put up with that. I tried to act as a boy, or a man. I don't know what they were expecting of me. I don't know how to walk that kind of walk they expected of me.

Yeah, but my father never reacted to me the way I was. My mom did though. But my father, I can't even remember a word or a single slap from my father, just because I expressed myself in a certain way as fa`afige. But I know my mom did, I used to get lashes from my mom because I expressed myself in certain ways. But I grew up in a chiefly family, my father's family; I was always in full potential of expressing myself as a fa`afafine. Although, I think because of that upbringing, my father never said anything to me. I think he respected me in that regard.

It's that fa`asamoa I grew up with, and that is reciprocity. And I thought, I have to return that respect, and I think that's why I don't dress up, because it's that mutual respect kind of spirit that I've had. But I know my mother; I have lived and believed in most of what she taught me as the right beliefs and values.

And I think just recently she accepted me as a fa`afafine when she found my diary; I was at second year at university and somehow she found my diary. And I remember I had every detail of everything I've done in my diary, including, you know, the boys I go out with and stuff. And she had a nervous breakdown. For a week she never talked to me. And that was the end of the diary book habit for me as well.

In the church, I know I come across many difficulties because

---

1 'Change and make right your walk or get your mouth slapped, okay?'

I was brought up in the LMS² beliefs and principles, so first of all I encountered a lot of bullying from the kids of the congregation at Sunday school gatherings. I always remember I was bullied, a victim of bullying at Sunday school. And also during school because the teacher, the Sunday school teacher would tell me, 'Why is your voice like that?' during the White Sunday occasions. 'Why are you sounding like a girl? Can you talk like a boy?'

I remember very well I never liked Sunday school and I never liked church. And I think from that day I started having negative understandings of the church and that upbringing. Up 'til now I hate LMS values and beliefs. And then I also moved to try and identify myself in the principles and values of the YFC, Youth for Christ, and evangelical movements in Sāmoa, and [there] also I went through the same thing: they would be saying, 'Now God doesn't love people like fa`afafine. Homosexuals is a sin, it's a sickness.'

It added on to my negativity view of God and Christianity. And since then I became rebellious of those beliefs. But because my family had established very basic values of, God loves you no matter what, you know, those personal relations with God; and, as I said before, it's often my mum who has been telling me, 'This is your relation with God.'

There was one time she would say to me, this is after the diary was found, she would say to me, 'You know, son, I don't want to see you in Hell. That's why I love you, and I hate the sin, I hate what you are fighting for, what you just expressed in your diary. But I love you and don't want to see you in Hell.'

And it was a turning point for me because, as you see, I read books, I'm a book lover, and I think it was more of a survival of the fittest for me. I think I had good friends, and, I don't know, I just find my way around and I struggled. To some extent I turned to my intellectual status as a fa`afafine. And my friends: fa`afafine friends, guy friends who are not homosexuals, girl friends who are not homosexual as well, I'm very privileged to have those

---

2 London Missionary Society, now the Samoan Congregational Church.

friends who surrounded me and kept me going, and some family members too. So, I think I'm one of those fittest that survived.

Mom used to give me those Bible stories, and I think she contributed to my like and love of reading. I remember when I was year seven, or year eight; the first book I got from the public library was *The Trojan Horse*. I remember I used to have a fantasy of those Greek goddesses and gods, those mythical creatures. From then on my love of reading led on to fantasies. I like the sorcerers, witches, wizards, and all that stuff. And just recently, I've started reading books as not romance, but murders and stuff. I also just started reading a book of a guy who used to be a professional diver and he was gay, and he won the world championship as a professional diver.[3] I'm matured and relating to books on finding yourself, finding your inner self.

As I said before, I was a victim of bullying, in Sunday school and including in my family, so I have been bullied, a real victim of bullying. In primary school I was exploring myself. I know when I got to year six, seven, eight, I started liking boys, and I was the victim of bullying until I went to college but then it got worse, it got worse. It started as a mild stage of bullying. I think the more I expressed myself as fa`afafine, the more bullying, the worse it becomes.

So it got to the stage where I became a victim of sexual abuse when I was at College. I remember I'd been asked to do a blowjob for one of the prefects. And there was also the time I was asked to do a hand job for one of the boys. These boys were older boys. I think because of my hatred, that hatred in me, and at the same time pressure from the family as well the church and Sunday school, because all these negative forces were on to me, I think from then on I find myself, I turn to things like books, and I turned to studies.

I was defenseless physically, because I'm not that kind of aggressive person but there was another force that sort of pushed

---

3 *Breaking the Surface* by gay Samoan diver Greg Louganis, who was adopted and raised by a Greek American family.

me, and that was hatred of these things. And the only way for me to retaliate, to come back, was through my education. You know, I fought my way through.

And I've seen most of those boys who were bullying me at Sunday school, I see them and they haven't gone anywhere! And I've gone somewhere. I said to myself, Look, this is my revenge; I am somewhere now; I have that content feeling. I have achieved something. And because I've achieved that, I'm now moving to another level of challenge, which is to fight for what my family was pressuring me about all the time – which is why I am now a human rights activist for LGBTI rights, including fa`afafine.

In education, I think, I'm privileged to have the support of my family, especially my father. He was very strict with our education and us. We used to have those faiga loku afiafi. And I know whenever my father asked, 'Faiga loku afiafi,' it means he's going to ask, 'What are your homework?', especially towards the end of the year. Usually I hated – it's one of those fears I had, apart from death – when it was after exams, waiting for reports from school. My father would usually call a special faiga loku. He would ask us about our reports, and he would look at the reports – it was the report from the teacher about us – and it's time for him to ask us about the report, and we will be answering him. And it was one of those horrific times. I think my father was behind us, behind me, and also because I'm the only one in my family who managed to go this far. None of my brothers and sisters went that far.

And that's why I'm saying, although my father contributed to it, it really came down to me: I had that spirit, that fighting spirit that was always within me, because of all these pressures from my family, from school, from Sunday school, from the church that I went to. I think it's that hatred – I don't think hatred is always bad – I think hatred as well made me survive. Anger. Anger in me, rebellious feeling, I think I managed to survive by that source of strength within me. I may be soft, I hardly speak, but I tell you I'm quite aggressive when it comes to issues involving fa`afafine, issues about LGBTI rights. Now I have achieved my status of standing above the people who used to abuse me, I managed to overcome that.

The next step for me is trying to fight something – those forces that had come into various phases, through my family, through my ministerial pastor – so I'm now going that far. Ever since I went to college I did research; I did research on fa`afafine, up to the stage where I investigated human rights. It took me to the stage where I thought the best way to do this is to be a lawyer. I had a shallow understanding of fighting for those rights; I thought it's always a lawyer who can do that. Then I just realised, you don't have to be a lawyer to fight that, you can be any kind of profession, an artist or whatever, and you can still fight that. I think it has to do with injustices and the various interpretations of what kind of person you are, that is the major force that drove me to where I am now.

The Crimes Ordinance of 1961 was one of those laws that were adopted directly by our Samoan government from the New Zealand administration. It survived the New Zealand Crimes Act 1961. And those provisions, section 58,[4] were copied directly from the New Zealand Crimes Act 1961 and applied to Sāmoa during the New Zealand administration. Then, when Sāmoa became an independent nation in 1962, that law was automatically applied as part of the independent Sāmoa. Samoans did not make those laws. They were made by the New Zealand administration who were at those times palagis.

At that time in New Zealand the issue of homosexuality was clearly, was acutely discriminated against and prohibited. The special provision about impersonation of females was not adopted from New Zealand; it was created by the New Zealand administration because at that time the fa`afafine were already seen in Sāmoa. They were already seen parading in town, and the New Zealand administration and government at that time thought to create that law only for Sāmoa because of the fa`afafine.

---

4 Regarding various issues, including homosexuality and transgenderism.

I'm going to give the reason why I think that was the case. There was a same provision in Vanuatu because during the French and British government, who were administering the governance of Vanuatu, they made a similar law that liquor – the selling of liquor – was not allowed to indigenous people, and the reason given was that the indigenous Ni-Vanuatu were always violent and drunk and stuff; so the same thing for Sāmoa, they created a particular law for the indigenous people. That was the real face of colonialism in those particular times. And the irony of that is that New Zealand has now moved forward ten steps ahead and Sāmoa has yet to amend those laws.

At this stage the Samoan government, in 2007/2008, established a new commission called the Sāmoa Law Reform Commission. The first task of the commission was to review some of the outdated laws, and one of those laws was the Crimes Ordinance 1961. Now the commission has called for public submissions in some areas of the Crimes Ordinance.

Samoan Fa`afafine Association Incorporated, which was one of the first associations to address issues of LGBTI, including fa`afafine issues, made submissions; and four members, including myself, made submissions on behalf of the Samoan Fa`afafine Association. Most of our submissions were to decriminalise or remove these laws: the prohibition against homosexuality should be removed absolutely, except with minors; and the law against 'the impersonation of a female by a male' should be removed absolutely as well.

Once a submission has been made to Parliament, it must be discussed by Parliament. Now these issues I've just mentioned, that we submitted on, are very sensitive issues in the Samoan culture. It's most likely it will be a hot debate in Parliament. We understand our prime minister is the patron of the Samoan Fa`afafine Association. And as the ruling regime of the government of the day, his party has the most votes. If they do vote for that the law changes we proposed, it will be thumbs up for our community. We are not arguing just because we want to be recognised in that respect; we are arguing because that's who we are. You know, it's our dignity. It's who we are. It's our status as such.[5]

There's never been a case of someone being charged under the impersonation law. Fa`afafine are allowed to roam freely in town, and in the villages as well. Even under the laws against homosexuality, there has never been a case submitted in a court in Sāmoa where two men above the age of consent have been charged with having sexual intercourse, even though it is clearly prohibited. There were cases brought to court where men had sex with a male under the age of consent. Now the law clearly states that having sex with a male under the age of consent is not consensual sex at all – and it is illegal.

But the reason we are arguing is it can be used as a way to blackmail the community. It's already a source of inciting violence in the future. Law enforcement may not implement that, but there are people – there will be homophobic people that will turn around and use it against the Samoan community. Plus, what's the point of it being there when they're not implementing it? It's a mockery to the main fabric of what the law should be. That's my humble understanding of why it needs to be removed.

I put myself as a victim of bullying and labeling; and verbal and sexual abuse, both in my family and outside of my family. And I tell myself that although I may have had bad experience of that and turned myself against my Christian beliefs and values, I still believe, I have a strong conviction of being Christian. And I know that my personal relationship with my God, who I know assisted me throughout the whole time, will always be there.

Regarding younger fa`afafine, I'm speechless of the question and I don't think I have the wise cap to advise other fa`afafine. But I would just say: the family – work within the family; this will provide the strength and energy to keep on. I would go back to basics: work within your family and you will be able to survive.

---

5   The Crimes Act of 2012 nullified these laws.

Iereneo Tauailauti Veavea
Photographer: Jean Melesaine

Iereneo Tauailauti Veavea

I'm the only son of my father and mother, Motu and Mauri, raised in San Francisco Bay Area. She was sent off-island and the marriage she had with my father was an arranged marriage. She came here, stayed with my aunt, Poiva, and they had a friend, who was a very good guy, was in the military, the air force, and was a bandleader. They set my mother and my father up, and that's how they became married. When he was retired he took us all back, we stayed in Sāmoa for one year; I was already Americanised so it was fascinating because it was like being in a big back yard, everything was green. We were considered the palagi kids because all we spoke was English. I went to an American English-speaking school in town in Fagatogo, American Sāmoa, 1966–67.

At that time the public TV pilot programs were happening, where we were sort of like guinea pigs: they would teach educational TV to the islanders. I remember being in a fale o`o and there was a TV there, it was the only TV that was there. A lot of the people would watch it, and they would try to imitate palagis. They would be speaking gibberish but they would think it was palagi. They would try to imitate the lady on TV.

I remember we had a lot of stuff; my father took the whole house, a container to the Islands, so we were like very well off in the eyes of the Islanders who were still living in fale o`o and cooking outside. My father used to beat my mother when he was drunk. Actually he was the most loving man I ever knew when he was sober, but when he was drunk we just kinda stayed clear. Same old story, he never beat me, only my mom, never my sister.

I remember him in the middle of the village of Nu`uuli playing his trumpet. He was a very different type of Samoan man. He always spoke to me in English. I'm not really fluent in

Samoan but if I'm comfortable around an elderly person I can speak it like there's no tomorrow.

He was an alcoholic. He would beat her all the time. The last time he beat her in Sāmoa for a mile and a half, all her clothes were ripped, and they found her purses and her shoes. He was very jealous, you know. She was very young. She wanted to live the American life. So she was working at the airport as a waitress in the coffee shop. And he always suspected her of infidelity because he was jealous; she was young, she was beautiful still.

So after he beat her, torn lip, broken nose, broken ribs, black eyes, her friends hid us out in Pago Pago until she became better, and then we fled. We fled Sāmoa, and we stayed with an aunt in San Francisco. And then she found a place in Sunnydale, which is a housing project of San Francisco and that's where I was raised.

I didn't see fa`afafine. Not that I was aware of. And that's the whole thing; some of my earliest sexual play in Sāmoa was actually with little girls. Never really saw any fa`afafine, but I knew they had to have been around. Looking back at it now, they probably were aunties, but I just ... it was never ... they never tripped off of it, or thought about it.

Funny thing is, when I thought I was gay or whatever, I thought I would have to become a woman. Because there was this movie that came out, the *Christine Jorgensen Story*,[1] and that was the only thing I had to relate to. So I was like, wow, so I have to get breasts and you know, the whole thing. So my whole demeanor started to change because that was the only thing I knew. Yeah, not much of a role model – not that there's anything wrong with it, because I wasn't like some transgenders who think they're not in the right body. I was comfortable with my body, I knew I liked my same sex, I just didn't know where to put it – where was I – and then this movie kinda came along and said, Well this is what you're supposed to do. And I was like, Shit,

---

1 A 1970 movie based on the 1960 autobiography by the first widely known American transsexual.

so I gotta pay for all this shit. I was thinking of ways, so how can I pay for this surgery, it was fucking crazy.

My mom, I think the reason why we were so close is because of her abuse by my dad. And to be honest with you, she was very abusive, if not physically, verbally, growing up, from the time we escaped his abuse, to hers. I would be called ugly, fat. 'You eat too much,' 'You're a fafafige,' or whatever! Whatever her issue was at the time.

It wasn't until I was a little older that I understood where all that came from, being a single mother, trying to raise two kids, working at a job that didn't really pay that much, not having support from her family because she left a quote-unquote 'good man' who provided for her.

Yeah, it must have been fricking crazy to try and feed two kids. Her only way of taking it out was taking it out on the eldest, which was I. When I came to peace with that, it made me love my mother even more. She didn't have the social services, a support system to say, 'Okay, you can't call your kid this, you can't hit your kid because of this.' So it was hard, it was really, really, really, hard for her. And later we became like the best of friends. I forgave her in my heart. It was like, 'If I had known that, when I was young when you were beating me ...' I mean there were some moments where I thought, Oh my God she's going to really kill me.

But now I look at her and I think there should have been someone there in our culture to intervene and say, 'You're going to be fine raising kids.' And especially in the sixties during a time when they already looked at her with, 'You're not White, you must be African American, you must be Negro.' She took the bus in the morning. She had a lot to endure. And she will always be my role model.

As a kid, I had the biggest crush on this little white kid. He would come over and we would, like, explore. And I was like, you know, when you're that young you don't think of it as being turned on, but I just knew, o-o-oh, this is it. But I always knew – after that there was no question – that I was ... I don't even think there was a word for it; I just thought it was kind of natural. It only became unnatural when people were giving me those negative images, not images but remarks like 'fafafige'. Fafafige was such a derogatory term in my family. Or 'Nancy'. I was like, 'Who the fuck is Nancy?' But they were always calling me Nancy: 'Do we have a relative named Nancy?' I guess that was a term for effeminate fafafige: 'Hey, Nancy!'

'Fafafige' was not a good term, and I don't want to say role models but drag queens, really effeminate – they were the seamstresses, or the caretakers, or whatever – and they'd always say, 'Yeah, you're going to be just like that.'

There was Seke, I remember Seke. And Puipui, Puipui I still know and love to death, I still see him; he's in his seventies. Puipui did anything he wanted to. He was just Puipui. I remember coming home from the clubs when I was older, it would be like 3:30, 4:30 in the morning. He would be this body sitting – and this is in America – on the side of the road in a pair of hotpants and a really fucked-up wig, and we'd roll up really slow because them other malas in the car, they'd be like, 'Oh my God, there's Pui.' And we'd kinda roll up really slow, and roll down the window, and in really deep voices say, 'Hey baby, where you going?'

And he'd turn his head and he'd look and he'd realise it was us and he'd throw his wig off. But he was well into his late forties, and we'd laugh, we'd be like, 'Uh, Pui, it is really cold out here, and you got like hot pants on.'

He'd get up and go, 'Get out of here!'

Yeah, Pui … But now he's really just a regular old man. But yeah, he was cruising, 3:30, 4:30 in the morning, we were coming back from the club, 'You're not cold?' But, yeah, so…

Here's the thing, we all experiment. And to me it was perfectly natural to lie up in the bed with another boy my age that might have been a family member or a friend of a family member. It just happened, and you always knew on the weekend you would get something. So it was good, it was all good.

It was the girls who … because I was also – and maybe that's why I have an issue with church – because there would be this group of girls who would lock me in the closet and they'd take turns making out with me, making me touch their private parts, both top and bottom. So if my hands weren't touching something, I was tonguing them. Yeah, this went on in our church. And you know what's really, really funny, when I see those women today – because we're all in our fifties and sixties – I try to be as feminine as I can, so they can be like, 'Oh my God and to think I was with him! I ruined that man for life!'

The seventies. Well, here's the really fortunate thing, even though my mother was a faife`au's kid, we were never forced to go to church – we basically found out about our spirituality on our own, while all my cousins were going to a structured church every Sunday. My cousins, they suppressed more and more their homosexuality, their gayness. And to this day, they're gay, but they just won't come out, because of the church.

Now, I'm not saying I never went to church. I have found churches, when I was there, to be very supportive of you as a family member, you as an individual; but once they start preaching on the pulpit about you're going to burn in Hell, God still loves you even though you're a homosexual but you can't live that deviant lifestyle, I would get up and leave and never turned back because, you know, why would I want to belong to something like that? You know, God loves you still but you're a freak of nature, kind of thing. So I never ... my mother would never force us to go to church. And that's why I think I'm a better off gay man today, than having to believe in all that bullshit they preach.

The history is, when I turned forty, forty-one, I was ready, and I always wanted kids. I mean, I raised family members' children, and I've always wanted kids. So when I turned forty-one, I picked up a phone, called home and said, 'Okay, I want a kid!' It was like an order, it was like takeout. And my aunt said, 'Okay. You want a boy or a girl?' And I was like, 'I don't care. I just want to be a dad.' She said, 'Okay,' and she hung up the phone.

Two weeks later, she was like, 'Oh, there's this girl, she is having a baby, she's too young, and so you better get ready and come and pick the baby up. She's going to have the baby soon.' I said, 'Okay.' I started buying cribs, and I was so excited.

So a week later, she called again, 'Okay, come pick up your baby.' I was like, 'What?' 'Oh yeah, she had a baby, she wanted him to be raised in the States.' I was, 'Okay, where's the baby?' She, 'Oh, the baby's here in my house.' I'm, 'What?' 'Oh yeah, they're very mad, I took the baby only four hours old.' I'm, 'You took the baby?' 'Yeah, but it's okay, I know the family.' I'm like, 'Are you going to get in trouble?' 'Oh, no, don't worry.' So I was like, 'Okay.'

So I immediately booked, I couldn't go because I was working, so I booked my mom's flight, and I gave her a thousand in pocket money, and sent her the next week to Sāmoa. And she got there, she called me, 'Okay, the baby's in my arms!' And I'm like, 'What?' And she's, 'Yeah, he's got a big mouth.'

So when she came from the airport, my mother, it was classic, she just walked off the airplane, she looked exhausted, she just swung the baby carriage to me, like passing a fruit basket, 'Here's your baby.' And I just looked at it, he looked at me, 'Oh my God, he's so ugly,' but I said it lovingly.

So yeah, that's how I came upon adopting a son. His name is Alesana, Sana. I was a pure daddy. The drugs stopped, the partying, the sex scene, I mean, I was a full-time dad. I boiled all his food, everything, I wanted to be a dad. I wasn't in a relationship, that didn't come until he was like three or four. Yeah, I was a solo mom. Yeah, I still worked, and I kept him with me.

My mother was like, 'Oh just leave him here.' I was, 'No, I'm the dad.' I worked at Cathedral Hill Hotel. His first New Year's was while I was working at the front desk, I had him at the front desk, people were checking in, 'Oh, how cute, a baby!' Yeah, we got a room there, and my niece would watch him. My mom was like, 'Leave him here.' 'No, I'm taking him with me. That's my baby!' She was like, 'What ever; wait 'til he becomes a teenager.'

Funny thing, Sana was ten and he started asking these questions. His adoption first, and after we cleared that up, he asked about being gay, 'Are you gay?' And I said, 'Yeah.' And he kinda said, 'Uh, am I going to be gay?' And we laughed. And I go, 'Not if you [don't] wanna be.' And he goes, 'No, I'm pretty sure no, I like girls.' I'm, 'Okay, well, that's fine.' But yeah, he's sixteen now, he has a girlfriend. I don't think he's gay; I don't care. I just want someone who's going to become a protective, loving, caring human being.

Well, my partner, Alex … So I am a busy dad, I didn't have time, a relationship was not in the picture. I just wanted sex, at that time the Internet, we couldn't afford a computer, and I don't think a lot of people were doing the Internet, so I put a sex ad out on the phone, just wanted to take care of business. So he kept on leaving messages, 'Oh, I'm eighteen, yadda, yadda, ya.' I'm like, 'I already have a son, I don't have time for another one, you know what I mean?'

So after the sixth message that he left, I'm, 'Oh let me call him.' And then I picked him up, he looked like a fifteen-year-old kid, he was in his baseball cap. I was forty-one, I told him I was thirty-five. I said, 'Can I see your ID?' He goes like, 'What?' I, 'Can I see your ID?' So he gave me his ID. He was nineteen. I was, 'Okay, well I'm not going to go to jail.'

He moved in four months later. It was like, I don't have no time to court you, you either move in or no. He just made me feel real comfortable. My mother didn't like him; my family didn't like him because he looked really young. And a lot of it too, now, I had never been in a relationship around my family. I was no longer available to cook, or go do functions with family, that's the way I saw it. I was spending my time with him, and with Sana, they were just like, 'Uh, we don't like him.' My mother would just say derogatory remarks like, 'Oh, your other son wants you,' because he was so young.

Because Alex is such a nurturing, caring person, he ended up winning my mother over big time. She would do things like give him money and say, 'Don't tell Neo' – those kinds of things – 'Go buy you something.' Like I'd been depriving him or something. Alex is a cook for the Marriott. He went to culinary school. That's another thing, I did kind of raise him.

About UTOPIA, in 1984, with Amisone McMullin, myself, Roy Muao, Julio Muao, Tane Fale, a bunch of Samoans, we got together because we were so proud of the fact that we were gay that we were going to march in San Francisco Gay Pride of 1984, and we'll call ourselves Gay Samoans – so that was our application form, 'Gay Samoans', and we marched; there were thirteen of us and a couple Latins, we made them look like Samoans, like Polys, because they were supportive. In my uncle's pickup truck, and a sound system, he didn't even know his pickup was being used for the parade.

The first time I said, 'We're going to create a gay march', Mom was like, 'Okay, I'm going too, I'll make the taco salad, you guys can use the garage' – there was not even the bat of an eye. And sure enough she made good on her word, she was cooking, and everyone felt really comfortable, it was the house to go to. And even her sister, we lived in a duplex, she came in and gave me thirty dollars to help us buy material for our little float.

A cousin from New Zealand came, he was here for two weeks, he was a huge bodybuilder kind of guy, so I said, 'Do you want to be in a parade?' He, 'Uh, I don't mind.' He was straight, and I went, 'Oh, you know it's fa`afafines', and it kinda went over his head, 'Is okay.' So he was on the back of the truck, he just looked very manly, very Samoan, and as the parade kept on going down he saw more and more naked people. His pale[2] went from, like, the back to over his eyes. He was only eighteen at the time, but he said he had the best time of his life.

So after that zooming to 1998, the same group of malas, plus more, Hawaiians and, well, we decided we needed to reorganise because there were so many of us out there. So Julio called me up, 'Can you organise the malas there? Let's call it UTOPIA, United Territories of Polynesians in Alliance.' We all chipped in two hundred dollars, all these malas, for the first parade, and out of those two hundred dollars we were able to do a picnic, and the word was out. All of a sudden I met all these different malas,

---

2 Headpiece made from flowers and leaves.

who were Tongan, Hawaiian, Fijian, Samoan, I was like, 'Oh my god.' The first gathering, I think it was like close to a hundred, so many gay people, and they brought their kids, and that's how we started to organise. And I became the first president. They all got involved, my family got involved, it was unreal.

Esta Noche was a gay Latino salsa bar back in the nineties and we Samoans ended up going there because it was the closest thing to a bar of color that we can go to, because they had closed down the African American bar that we used to go to. The Castro was much too white because we'd go in there, it took forever for them to serve us a beer, we kinda got the clue they didn't want us down there. Esta Noche was opening with welcome arms; it was the Latino community. It was a dive bar; when we would walk in, they'd usually play modern music, once in a while they'd play salsa music, or Celia Cruz, then we'd walk in: they'd play 'Tahiti Tahiti', that disco version, everyone would look like, Oh here come the Islanders. We were basically all Samoan, they'd all make a circle, we'd be fake-assing this Tahitian number that we do. That was it, every time we walked in you'd hear, 'Ia orana, orana,' here we are these Samoan queens dancing with pride then. I think that was the only Poly music that was out, you know like, club music. So we all danced to it. That was Esta Noche.

The Pendulum,[3] when the P started, everyone started hanging out at the P. I became the president of UTOPIA, and my philosophy was, I couldn't really party with the members because I wanted respect, I wanted to make sure when I said something that they listened to me, not, 'Oh that bitch was drunk last night she don't know what she's talking about.' But the P was the place to go, they played my kind of music, R&B, very funky, and if you knew the words you were singing it at the bar. The clientele was predominantly African American and those who loved them. Some white guys would be in there. And a lot of Samoans and Tongans and Hawaiians went there because, then again, we felt

---

3 Former gay African American club in The Castro in San Francisco, also called The P.

welcomed. We felt it was a part of us, we're a people of color, we know what it's like, and they even named a drink after us, 'Hot Cousins' – we were called hot cousins, cause we were like cousins, and we were hot.

Some of our members were there five days a week, they lived in that bar; drinking in the community, there's too much of it, and drugs. I'm no angel. But some people stay like they were in their twenties, drinking every day, gotta have a beer, gotta have some wine, by the time they go to an event, they're smashed. Nobody seems to want to address it; it's like, 'Oh that's his or her problem.' And let's not talk about meth, I think it's still out there, and I'm no angel, I used it too, it was a recreational drug. When my son came along I quit. I used to do it every weekend, I kept my house clean, and I put my money aside for that. But like I say, my son came along, it was cold turkey, there was no question in my mind. I couldn't do that shit anymore – I can't stay up the whole weekend and expect to take care of some kid who's going to be screaming and crying – so yeah, he was a godsend in many ways.

When I got diabetes I thought I would never live without rice but it causes your blood sugar to spike, it's almost like a drug. I've been three years without and I don't miss it. I contracted that disease from food issues, eating way too much. There would be times we'd be up at two in the morning and company would come over and I'd be cooking a full meal, chicken, rice, veggies, salad, we'd all sit down and just laugh and eat, 4:30 comes rolling around and everybody goes to sleep, wake up in the morning at nine or ten and have a big ass breakfast, God forbid it should be a little crepe on a plate. As far as eating and diabetes, I've learned to portion control, and with drugs and everything else.

When I began noticing HIV, I'm sure we had the mentality, 'That won't happen to us, it only happens to white people, we're strong, and we don't get those kinds of diseases.' But when it started impacting more than just white people, then a lot of these queens, a lot of these gay men started to get scared. But it taught me a lesson to see the reaction of my friends and stuff, they had already written me off that I had HIV, these were gay friends, and it was only because of the fear, we didn't know.

Early eighties, every time somebody got sick there was speculation, 'Oh, `o ma`i, they got AIDS.' And sure enough a couple of friends contracted it. Roy[4] passed away of HIV. Later – I think because there was such a big influx of education going into the gay community, and also in the general public at large, that living with HIV wasn't really the issue anymore – it was how do you help them cope with HIV ... a lot of the fear had come down.

But in the early days of it, we still say it to this day, a whole segment of gay men were wiped out in the Castro. Now, you look at the Castro, it is not the same as it was back in the heyday. Now there are a lot of straight families with babies, a lot of people of color there, it's different. Those men who all passed if they were still alive today would be my age. Mid fifties, early sixties, it would be a whole different community.

I grew up in and around Visitacion Valley. It's changing; at one time it was predominantly African American. At one time, there was a lot of crime here; a lot of people didn't want to come to this part of the neighborhood. There's still a large population of African Americans and Samoans, but the Asian community and the Latino community outnumber them now. I know, growing up, when someone would say to me, 'Oh, you're my brutha, we're bruthas,' I would automatically be insulted by a meauli, by a black person, when they said that to me, because of the stigma. My parents put that on me. They didn't know any better; it was stigma they learned from the people in this country that black people were bad. So we were just one step better than them, we were high yellow Samoans. So I believed that hype, whenever a black person was trying to get close to me when I was younger, I was, 'Oh my god, I'm not like you.' But when I grew up I knew better. I am like them. Because I'm

---

4 Roy Muao 1959–2004, co-founder of UTOPIA San Francisco with brother Julio Muao.

looked at the same way they're looked at through the eyes of other people. I guess I have become the advocate for the African American people here, because there is an exodus of them, and people don't know why they're leaving, but hell, they're leaving because you're not making it any better for them to stay. And if they leave, that means we leave, because we're next.

May is National Asian Pacific Islander Heritage Month in San Francisco. Malia Cohen our district supervisor said that, 'Neo Veavea is a leader in the Samoan community.' And I thought, Wow, I am? Because I never really do a lot of work in the Samoan community, I do the work in my community – not Samoan specific, just wherever I'm needed. But I guess you can say I'm doing it outside of the box, I'm not necessarily doing it in the Samoan community, but I am a representation of the Samoan community.

Fa`afafine associations

Sāmoa Fa`afafine Association (SFA)
The Independent State of Sāmoa

SOFIAS Sosaiete o Fa`afafine i Amerika Sāmoa
American Sāmoa

Love Life Fono
Aotearoa New Zealand

UTOPIA Hawai`i, New York, San Diego, San Francisco, Seattle
and Washington DC
United States

About the editors

Dan Taulapapa McMullin

Dan Taulapapa McMullin is a poet and painter, with work in various media. His book of poems *Coconut Milk* was in the Top Ten LGBT Books of the Year of the American Library Association. He was the recipient of a Poets & Writers Award, and residencies from the DeYoung Museum, Jerome Foundation, McKnight Foundation, California Arts Council, and American Sāmoa Arts and Humanities Councils. He has presented work at the Metropolitan Museum, Auckland Art Gallery and the Bishop Museum. His 2017 appropriation film *100 Tikis* is screening internationally, and he is currently working on a novel. www.taulapapa.com

Yuki Kihara

Yuki Kihara is an interdisciplinary artist whose work engages with a variety of social, political and cultural issues. Kihara critically engages with Pacific colonial history and representation as it intersects with race, gender and sexual politics. The Metropolitan Museum of Art presented a solo exhibition of Kihara's work entitled Living Photographs (2008) featuring highlights of her art practice, followed by an acquisition of her works by the museum for their permanent collection. Her works are also in the collections, among others, at The Los Angeles County Museum of Art, The British Museum and Te Papa Tongarewa Museum of New Zealand.

Acknowledgments

Fa`afetai tele lava, thank you, from the Editors to the following for their kind help in the completion of this book: Creative New Zealand Arts Council and the Government of New Zealand for travel funds; University of California, Los Angeles, Postcolonial and Literary Studies Group for transcription services. And for their invaluable advice and guidance at various phases of this project: Momoe Malietoa Von Reiche, Dionne Fonoti, Rosanna Raymond, Sia Figiel, Elizabeth DeLoughrey, Stephen Dunn, and especially Evotia Tamua, Tony Murrow, and Amy Tansell at Little Island Press. Many thanks go to Lana Shields, Fernandez Matai, and all the family members who donated photographs. And to our families, who helped us in the making of this book, alofa atu.

www.ingramcontent.com/pod-product-compliance
Lightning Source LLC
Chambersburg PA
CBHW030835270326
41928CB00007B/1071